Gstaad
Insider's Guide

People / Places / Shops / Hotels
Restaurants / Schools / Culture
Sport / Business / Excursions

Farrol Kahn

Farrol Kahn

Farrol Kahn is a journalist and author of aviation health and travel books. His books on flying include Curse of Icarus (Routledge 1990); Why Flying Endangers Your Health (Aurora Press 1992); Airwise (C W Daniel 1993); Arrive in Better Shape (Harper Collins UK 1994 & US editions 1995). The travel books have covered Oxford (Landmark 2005) and Riga & its Beaches (Landmark 2007)

His current book The Insider's Guide to Gstaad follows his trio on Lake Geneva which includes Montreux Riviera, Lausanne and Geneva.

The others cover the Valais - the undiscovered canton and Crans Montana, which has the cleanest air in Switzerland.

Published by Valais Books
Farrol Kahn GmbH, Ritz und Partners,
Bahnhof Strasse 19
3904 NATERS
Switzerland
Tel: +41 (0) 79 568 2842

Printed by Gutenberg Press Ltd.
Gudja Road
Tarxien
Malta GXQ 2902

Design and layout AZZZA Limited, UK
Picture Editor: Anja Meier

ISBN 978-3-9524208-5-0

Email: farrol.kahn@bluewin.ch

Acknowledgements

To all the people I had pleasure of interviewing for the book.
To my muse.
To AZZZA who I've enjoyed working with again.
To my Picture Editor, Anja Meier.
To Christine Camerana, a dining companion.
To everyone who participated in the photo competition.

Photo Credits: There are numerous sources for photographs including my own. A big thanks to the Gstaad Saanenland Tourismus which has one of the best selection of photos of all the Swiss destinations. Gstaad Saanenland Tourismus. Thanks also to Stephan Jaggi architect, Raphael Faux, Grand Chalet Robert Mühlbacher, Ombretta Ravessoud Sommets Musicaux de Gstaad, Ruedi Hählen, Pierre Genecand & Hublot Polo Gold cup, Nachson Mimran, Pascale Heuberger, Prof Nasser David Khalili, Antonia Crespi, Mehran Azmoudeh, Urs Hodler, Bernhard Nicod, Irene Kung, Dariane Pictet, Toni von Grünigen, Andrew and Gabriele Braunsberg, Richard Scarry, Dominique Rossignol-Franck, Walter Egger, Bethli Kung-Marmet, Manrico Iachia & the Gstaad Yacht Club, Christine Camerana, Stephan Romang, Delice, René Ryser, Patricia Low/Jeff Koons, Christoph Romang, Pascale Heuberger, Antonella, Marina Anouilh, Urs von Unger, Giovanella, Andi Stricker, The Alpina Hotel, Andrea Scherz, HUUS Hotel, Bruno Kernen, Tommy Oehrli, Romantik hotel Hornberg, Sonnenhof Restaurant, Grand Chalet, Lac Renaud/Franz Wehren, ESV. CH/Schwingen, Manuel Blanco/Credit Suisse, JürgVon Allmen/Saanenbank, Müller Medien, Hans-Ueli Tschanz, Addor AG, Karin Mösching, Jaggi Architecture/Elisabeth Wampfler, Philippe Warren/ Armin Wehren, Michael Tschanz, Tom Galler/Galler AG, Gstaad Menuhin Festival, Christoph Müller, Renaud Capuçon, J. Safra Sarasin Swiss Open Gstaad, Eagle Ski Club and Anita Roth-Reuteler. A big thanks to the competitors of the photo competition: Evelyne Petten, Stefan Jaggi, Hannes Schlögelhofer, Karin Bach, Regula Hauswirth, Corinna Müller, Nadia Reichenbach, Rainier Donker, Francesca Herrmann, Pascal Bangerter, Kathrin Frautschi, Elizabeth Riordan, Janine Buchs, Hans Bernasconi, Annekäthi Zingre, Deborah Walker, Franz Rosskogler, Maria Rieder, Daniela Giessbühler, Andy Kuenzi, Sabine Reichenbach, Uta Merzweiler, Tanja Coulter.

Contents

Introduction 13

Chapter 1. **Who's Who:** People who reflect the dynamic spirit of the region. 17

Chapter 2. **Bakers.** Great homemade bread and mouthwatering patisserie. 79

Chapter 3. **Shopping.** Big brands to die for and great local discoveries. 85

Chapter 4. **Accommodation.** Finest selection of hotels in Canton Bern: from family run luxury to cosy, comfortable and beds in the oldest beautiful chalet. 115

Chapter 5. **Eating.** Watch the cows while you eat in a barn or quaff champagne in rustic alpine hut at 1,400m while a top chef cooks meat on a spit or taste unforgettable cuisines in multi-starred restaurants. 133

Chapter 6. **Banks & Business.** How to get more bang for your bucks, whether buying a property or car, sponsorship, experiences, archiving or publishing. 143

Chapter 7. **Real Estate.** Locals that deliver Gold standard chalets, renovate farmhouses with several storeys below with swimming pools, gyms and car collections, demolish buildings and sell your houses worldwide. 157

Chapter 8. **Farming.** The 700 year-old tradition: Cows, goats and cheese. 171

Chapter 9. **Entertainment.** Anyone for tennis, polo? What about country or classical music? 177

Chapter 10. **Schools.** Local yokel or exclusive JFK education. 197

Chapter 11. **Guides.** She, a former flight attendant guides locally and he, a mountain guide who climbed the Eiger and is renowned for off-piste skiing. 203

Chapter 12. **Photo Competition.** Places we love! People from all walks of life, locals and foreigners from 17-71 participated in a photo competition.
The results of the winners were glorious. 207

Index 237

PARFUMERIE

Posthotäll Rössli heißt diz Hus
Seht sufer och inwändig us
Hät gräbta Wyn u. gueti Choscht
Chum inha gschwind –
– u. bschtäll was d' woscht.
CAFÉ RESTAURANT

The coats of arms in Saanenland.

Introduction

Gstaad was put on the tourist map after the railway line of the Montreux-Oberland-Bahn (MOB) was built (1904-1905). The visitors were attracted to Château d'Oex but the farmers who had been made wealthy from their Etivaz cheese did not want them. Instead, they send them to Gstaad where the farmers were poor..

But it was after the construction of the Palace hotel in 1913 that tourism got underway in the resort. It was followed by opening of Chalet Marie José, a private boarding school for girls and in 1919, Le Rosey created a winter campus. (See entries, Prince Michel, Evelyne Peten and Le Rosey)

Unknown facts about Gstaad: There are 7,000 cows and 7,000 people in the area. All the cheese is lactose free.

God's Fingers on Gstaad

Gstaad is the ultra chic ski resort which is mostly known for its glamorous après-ski and those who don't ski. Located in Bern Canton, it teems with the beautiful people who make it famous as one of the most exclusive resorts in Switzerland. During the peak season such as Christmas the highlight is the parade of elegant men, women, the wannabes and the gawkers along the Promenade - the Bond Street of London or Madison Avenue in New York. The luxury brands are showcased in carefully renovated century-old chalets which is a signature of Gstaad and several other villages in Saanenland. The village is easily recognisable because the fairy tale Gstaad Palace watches over it.

Gstaad has welcomed A-listers ever since the playboy Gunter Sachs and Brigette Bardot walked their dog down the Promenade in 1967. Audrey Hepburn, Grace Kelly, Liz Taylor, Richard Burton and Roger Moore all followed and it's the home of Roman Polanski, Valentino and Dame Julie Andrews who was made an honorary citizen in 2014.

The decoration on the masterpiece chalet - Drogerie Jaggi, Saanen (See page 107). Amazing discovery are the two magical squares (one is shown) to protect the building from disasters like fires or floods.

However, the success of the resort is attributed to the two communities living side by side in harmony and in respect of each other's privacy. Local children are taught not to make a fuss when they see famous people in the village. "Just treat them respectfully as they want their peace and quiet," they are advised.

The locals include the shopkeepers, hoteliers, restaurateurs, carpenters, bakers, butchers electricians and dairy farmers who march their cows through the village on, August 31 from the Alpine pastures every year. It is called Züglete or transhumance. Both communities enjoy a six month tourist-free period when the region reverts to them. The inhabitants can pick up things where they left off. Gstaad is like going to Neverland and dropping off never to return. But you won't find Peter Pan or Wendy there nor Peter's gang the Lost Boys in Kensington gardens. Rather hills and Alps and cows and villages with wooden chalets and farm houses. And sometimes animals like the shy chamois and the roe deer in the distance. The people, mostly farmers make cheese in the summer in cauldrons over a fire. In winter, they tend to become ski teachers and take to the slopes.

Families such as Bach, Baumer, Brand, Frautschi, Romang and Reichenbach were first recorded in the region in 1312. In all, there are 70 families each with their own coats of arms. It is likely that one of the Fleutis decorated the Saanen St Maurice church as their design of their coat of arms consists of a hand holding an artist's easel. (See entry, Karin Bach)

Sometime in their history they realised that it was a special place. Their legend which is still taught at school reminds one of a sort of Genesis. When God wanted to take a short rest while creating the earth he held onto it. The imprint of his hand thus shaped the Saanenland region. His five fingers formed the valleys, with Gstaad nestling in their midst. The little finger is Chalberhöni, the next finger is Feutersoey and Gsteig, the middle finger is Lauenen, the fourth finger is Turbach and the thumb is Schönried.

Other unique features of the Gstaad include the most exclusive school in the world Le Rosey and the Eagle Ski Club. The former spends its winter term in the village. (See entry, Le Rosey). A special train moves virtually everything from furniture to bedding, stationery to office and sports equipment as well as personal belongings from Rolle in Vaud to Gstaad. Then there's long weekend gathering in February when thousands descend on the village.

The Eagle Ski Club has too put Gstaad on the radar since it was founded in the late 1950s and together with the Palace hotel and Le Rosey are the main drivers of success of the resort. It has attracted celebrities, royalty, film stars and A-listers as members. Essentially, it is an exclusive dining club which focuses on skiing. Gstaad extends to satellite villages of Saanen, Schönried, Saanenmöser, Feutersoey and Turbach all of which are known as Saanenland plus the two outsiders, Gsteig and Lauenen which have their own municipalities. Overall the area is located at altitudes of between 1,000 and 1,400 metres. Despite its style and high-end reputation, Gstaad has retained its Alpine authenticity and is down-to-earth. The people are proud of their traditions and an economy based on cheese and the sale Saanen goats.

The municipality is based in Saanen which is a showcase of the chalet architecture and the masterpiece is Haus Drogerie Jaggi, Dorfstrasse 54. (See entry, Drogerie Jaggi). It was built in 1693 and was one of the most expensive buildings in the 17th century. The chalet is owned by Peter and Hans Jaggi and has three living rooms on the first floor. On the outside is a long inscription about the medieval owners - Hans and Melchior Strehl and the carpenter, Christian Tüller. The eaves are painted and has the only magical squares found on the chalets - a symbol with letters which were like gargoyles to protect the house against evil and dangers such as flood and fire.

Then the 2nd floor with 1 or 2 bedrooms known as "Gade", and above the attic which included a special room for storage. The entrance of the house was through the kitchen which had an open fire for cooking and an enormous chimney for smoking meat. The warmth provided by the stove in the living room reached the upper floor through holes in the ceiling.

For a comprehensive view of the traditional craft, the alpine farming and life in a medieval village, visit the Landwirtschaft museum.

Landwirtschaft museum
Dorfstrasse 64,
Saanen
Tel 033 744 79 88.

Chapter 1. Who's Who

People who reflect the dynamic spirit of the region.

'Connect Man' with 3,000 Contacts

The genius behind the sport of kings is **Pierre Genecand**. He takes life at a triple gallop and his interests span two continents - Europe and South America (Argentina and Uruguay). His great success with the International Horse Show (CSI) in Geneva from 1990 to 2003 speaks for itself. He had over 32,000 spectators in the last year of his involvement. For a man who lacks academic qualifications, his business model is certainly worthy of a case study by Harvard Business School, IMD or INSEAD.

Pierre Genecand

"I'm very curious about everything," said Pierre Genecand, a mild-mannered and amicable man. "I read fifteen newspapers a day and to have 220 TV channels at home. As a child, I hated school and was expelled from many institutions. I dreamed of traveling to get to know the world. But if there was anything I was passionate about, it was horses and I began riding at an early age. Later, I followed horse shows worldwide."

Although, Genecand's ideas of a career veered towards animal husbandry, his parents discouraged him from even owning a horse. His father ran Gesrep AG, the oldest insurance brokerage in Switzerland. After studying English in London and German at Mannheim, he joined him at 19. When his father died at 58 in 1982 after two heart attacks, he took over Gesrep AG. He built the business from 12 employees to 98 and eventually sold it in 2005 to the Dutch insurance giant AON.

"I started working for my father not as his right arm but as a simple typist," he said smiling. "I was on the typewriter eight hours a day for a salary of CHF 300 francs a month."

"It gives you character. I also began filling my notebooks with addresses which came to good use many years later."

Rides Six Horses Daily

He was the organiser of the CSI for 14 years and had moved from the small Les Vernets hall to the Palexpo exhibition centre. Then the horse enthusiast was asked by Brigitte Schaerer and her husband who was the general manager of the Gstaad Palace to take over the Hublot Polo Gold Cup Gstaad. (See separate entry, Gstaad Palace). Since then, the event has taken off. He has always enjoyed creating and organising events. This talent together with a passion for breeding horses, has always driven him. Today, he spends time between Uruguay, Argentina and Switzerland.

"As a former show-jumper, horse-riding was never an obstacle for me," he said. "In 2001 I became an ardent polo player. The king of games fascinates me because of its pace, the horses' incredible performance and the rapid side changes. I have been a team patron four times in Geneva and Zurich, and have played in Gstaad and St Tropez several times."

"My character traits include thoroughness and doing the right thing," he continued. "This has resulted in the lack of enemies. But I hate having to repeat the same thing twice and I don't support people who lack dynamism or are not motivated. So, in my daily activities, professional or sporting I'm surrounded by quality people and delegate a lot."

Genecand who learnt skiing in Schönried at 12, has a chalet in Gstaad. He has two daughters, one of whom, Veronique, was a show jumper for 10 years. He does at least one trip a year with his daughters as he wants them to see the world.

He is the perfect embodiment of the Latin phrase, men sana in corpora sano, a healthy mind in a healthy body. He does not drink alcohol and has never smoked. He rises at 6 am and practices one sport every day such as tennis, golf or walking. If its polo, he rides six horses in the morning to train and then in the afternoon plays matches. In his campo in Argentina, he has around 40 horses ready to play.

"My philosophy is never to buy something if you don't have the money," he said. "Wait until you have the amount you need. You're finished if go the a bank or use credit. To follow your dream you don't necessarily need to go to university. If you do sport you'll find out a lot of things about yourself."

He is known as "Connect Man" by his friends and proof of this was when the technician transferred his address book from one smartphone to another there were some 3,000 addresses. He is a master of networking and combines his passion of sport with business. It's inevitable when he's asked about his work and answers insurance - in all its forms from pensions to asset management that stimulates interest.

Lorenz Bach

Farmer and Fashionista

Lorenz Bach is a member of one of Gstaad's oldest farming families who can trace his ancestors back to the 14th century. He is also a haute couture entrepreneur who enticed the big fashion brands into the resort whereas before in the late 1970's the shops on the Promenade were cheesemongers, butchers and fruit and vegetable sellers.

Dairy farming is in his DNA and he runs two farms at Meielesgrund and Etivaz. His herds comprise Holstein cattle and the farms are medium-sized with some 35 cows. They produce three round cheeses a day at the beginning of the season when the pastures are rich then two towards the end when the grazing thins out. The best cheese is right at the start of the season. Like most farmers he has a favourite cow which is called Goldriana and was a winner in Switzerland's top bovine beauty pageant in 2014.

"I'm a farmer at heart," he said. "As a boy I spent my summers in the Bernese alps helping my father Hans. One of my tasks was milking cows by hand - before electronic milking machines were available. I also assisted in cheesemaking moving the harp to separate the curd from the whey. At the time, it took several hours of climbing to reach Meielesgrund.

Nowadays, I go up with my private cable car which is big enough to carry bales of hay and some dozen round cheeses which weigh 10 kg each. I always marvel at the spectacular views as we travel up or down."

Lorenz Bach always had a passion for being an entrepreneur and honed these skills as a boy of 10 when he bred goats and sold them. He was close to his father who instilled in him the maxim: "making a profit is easier than working hard." From then on, he appreciated that the brain was superior to the brawn.

Princess Diana

"I've seen the village change in the 1980's from being a skiing resort to a meeting place," he said. "At the age of 16, I became a skiing instructor and one of the people I taught was Queen Fara Dibah and her son Ali-Reza. It was fun because when we skied there were two bodyguards in front of us and at the back. Later, I travelled to South America and Aspen, Colorado on skiing trips."

His first venture into retailing was to start the Silver Sport ski shop in Rougemont in 1978. He chose well because there was no other competition, the rent was low and the village was also the site of the finishing school Alpin Insitut Videmanette which was an all girls institution where they were taught skiing, cooking, dressmaking and French. Princess Diana and Tamara Mellon were among the students.

"I shared the space with Dior and a fur retailer," he said. "But soon I was doing well and took over Dior and introduced other famous brands. However, when these brands did well they later opened their own shops. So by accident, I was responsible for changing the face of the Promenade, which today is filled with high-end shops."

At the age 25, Lorenz opened his first luxury fashion boutique, Maison Lorenz Bach, to cater to the needs of the resorts' glamorous and discerning clients. This was followed by another boutique, Bach signature, in Gstaad. Today, he has 21 shops in Switzerland including Silver Sport and luxury fashion boutiques.

"My clothing brand is defined as being casual chic or mountain chic," he said, "and can be worn anywhere. Essentially, I look upon it as a souvenir from Gstaad."

The Lorenz Bach SA is a private company and in 2003, he was offered a buyout but he was not interested in selling. He has five children, two of whom are involved in fashion - the eldest son runs the Silver Sports and his daughter is studying fashion. The other two sons are interested in farming while the youngest is only 10. His philosophy for the younger generation Is: "there is always a solution and use your brain rather than physical strength to solve it."

Nachson Mimran

Repair the World

Nachson Mimran is the chairman of the Grand hotel Alpina and co-founder with his brother Arieh of an impact investing company, TO: aka Tikkun Olam - Repair the World.

He is true to his Biblical name Nachson who was the brave leader of the Judah tribe and the first to enter the Red Sea in spite of any danger. This is exactly what he is doing in the 21st century as he plays a leading role as a creative activist who collaborates with individuals, artists, ventures and non-profits to create a sustainable world and to empower communities worldwide.

"TO: isn't so much a foundation as a laboratory - a place for innovation and engagement," he said on the launch of the magazine re;source in 2018. "One of our core beliefs is that business can and must help heal the world. That's how the Alpina Gstaad fits into the picture as a key launchpad for our initiatives. The property is a testing ground for things we believe in - as well as platform for inviting guests from around the world to experience our valued causes. We hope that re;source will give you a test of the art, the activations, the campaigns, the events close to our hearts . Perhaps, you'll join the journey."

There are initiatives galore like the many stars you see when you're hit between the eyes. The co-creating ventures range from ShadowmanVan, #togetherband, Light to

Learn, Leonardo DiCaprio Foundation Action Fund, Center for Sustainable Finance (UZH) to Co-Impact. The ventures vary from Beyond Meat, Bottletop, Bridge International Academies to L (toxin free condoms), Omaze, Runa and Samasource, Sunna Design and Terrafertil.

"The defining moment in life was in 2013, the year my mother died and my Tech business failed," he said. "It was then that I realised that I'd been selfish with my goals and wanted to support individuals and organisations making the world a better place. I had been a privileged young individual but had a duty and responsibility to share resources with talented communities around the world. I wanted to make a difference and give them an opportunity as talent is equally distributed but opportunity is not."

Prophet of Impact Economics

Nachson was born in Geneva and grew up between Europe and Senegal in West Africa where father, Jean Claude Mimran had developed an agri-business and was nicknamed the Sugar king. The family pioneered sustainable farming practices on their land which comprised 12,000 hectares, of which 8,000 hectares was sugarcane. The community grew from a 1,000 to 100,000 people and at least one member was employed by the Mimrans. Nachson was educated at Le Rosey and later gained a Bachelor in Business Administration at Westminster university, London. He is married to Natalia and they have three children.

"I was introduced to Gstaad by Le Rosey's winter term," he said, "It's a destination of peace, inspiration and natural beauty, and synonymous with forward thinking. I believe Gstaad can be a hub for this kind of attitude. There's going to be a shift in the next 10 years in which millennials will be in the forefront. But I think the destination should always maintain a 80:20 mix of preserving tradition with only 20% evolving."

To describe Nachson as a creative activist is incomplete. He is much more. He has the charisma of a rock star and has talent like the artist-entrepreneur Andy Warhol. In the future he will become the prophet of impact economics.

Good Design is Forever

There are interior designers and interior designers but few pass the muster of the profession. **Pascale Heuberger** is one who does and is a decorator extraordinaire. She was fortunate as she had a good start because she was brought up in a beautiful house with a beautifully manicured garden by her mother. Such environment honed her sense of aesthetics. In addition, she was introduced to the world of design in New York where she had a job in the famous fabric company Brunschwig & Fils.

"I am pleased that we have been entrusted with major projects and have clients in Gstaad, Zurich and London, a powerhouse of design," said Pascale who is fun, tall and elegantly dressed and yet has the Swiss precision. "I was proud when I was given a carte blanche to decorate a brand new chalet from scratch. I worked in collaboration with a fantastic team of local architects and craftsmen for a over a year without any consultation with the client. Every detail whether it was the kitchen design, bathrooms or lighting and of course all the furnishings was left to my imagination. It was terrifying as I'd been given a huge responsibility and had to rely on my own judgment. Then came the day of reckoning when I showed the client the results. To my relief and delight he responded, 'I take my hat off to you.'"

She celebrated that night with great bottle of a 2009 Pomerol, her favourite. The four storey chalet was built to house the clients' guests. It was high water mark in her business, Rougemont Interiors, which had been established in Greenwich, Connecticut in 2006. Today, it consists of her elegant store and design studio in Gstaad which includes a coffee shop on the Promenade.

"My passion for interior design started in my early 20s and while I worked, I imported Italian furniture for my colleagues and friends," she said. "I'd grown up surrounded by beautiful things me and wanted to create beautiful homes for others. Like Zelena Brunschwig, I believe that good design is forever."

Pascale was born in Bern and came to Gstaad with the family and friends. She liked to ski on the Wasserngrat and the favourite après ski place for the "Berners" was the Olden. She gained her commercial diploma and worked in marketing for a pharmaceutical and a hospital group. Later, she went to New York where she got married and had two children. After 10 years of living abroad, she returned back to her roots.

Pascale Heuberger

Gun Metal Grey

"Our uniqueness is that I only have very exclusive items in the shop and work with top craftsmen," she said. "As a real Swiss we work within budget, deliver on time and offer mostly turnkey solutions. The most rewarding thing about my job is when families come to Gstaad afterwards and remark how lucky they are to have a beautiful, cosy home to come back to every year."

"It's very important to understand your client," she continued. "What defines them, what I see to catch their personality. An example is an apartment I decorated for a single man. It was masculine, sober yet very elegant with finest materials. The sofa was in dark brown velvet, armchairs in leather with matching brass armrests. When I discovered that he had a motorbike, I added finishes in gun metal grey."

Nasser David Khalili

Healing The World with Art

Call him a latter-day Renaissance man, a polymath or simply a genius or what you will because Professor **Nasser David Khalili** - referred to by FIRST Magazine as "the Medici of the 21st century" – has blazed a trail in his life that no one has ever encountered. He is a mega-collector of world art and is the only billionaire whose fortune derives predominately from art.

Moreover he is a philanthropist, a real estate investor, founder of an interfaith charity and a world-renowned scholar of the history of art. But it would be reasonable to settle for genius. After all, he wrote a book about the 233 geniuses in the world when he was just 14 years old. Also he conforms to the definition of a genius by another author, Isaac D'Israeli, the father of the Prime Minister D'Israeli who wrote a book on the men of genius which he defined as "native intellectual power of an exalted type." (*The History of The Men of Genius,* published in 1818).

"The greatest and one of the strongest bridges between cultures is the one that is built out of art," said David Khalili, an energetic, affable and articulate man. "Religion and politics have their own languages; but the language of art is universal. This universality is what I represent and promote. What I set out to do is to concentrate on eight distinct areas where art had been overlooked. Gradually, over a period of five decades, I managed to awaken eight sleeping giants."

His collections are divided into Islamic Art, with artefacts dating from 700 to 2000; Hajj and the Arts of Pilgrimage from 700 to 2000; Aramaic Documents from 535 BC to 324 BC; Japanese Art of the Meiji Period from 1868 to 1912; Japanese Kimonos from 1700 to 2000; Swedish Textiles from 1700 to 1900; Spanish Damascened Metalwork from 1850 to 1900 and Enamels of the World from 1700 to 2000. Together, they comprise some 35,000 works of art, many of which have been exhibited at prestigious museums and institutions worldwide. Each work of art has been meticulously conserved, researched, catalogued and published as part of what is considered to be one of the most ambitious art scholarship projects in modern history. Seventy-two of over a hundred planned volumes have already been published, led by David Khalili and with contributions from the world's leading experts in each respective field.

Nasser David Khalili was born in the Iranian city of Isfahan to a family of Mizrahi Jews. David was exposed to art and Islamic artefacts at an early age because his father was a trader in these objects. From the age of eight he began to accompany him on buying trips over a number of years. When he was a teenager he was given his first piece, a 19th century Qajar lacquer pen box (which remains in his collections), by a collector who spotted the enthusiasm in the young Khalili's eyes. After completing his service as a medic in the Iranian army, he left in 1967 for the US to study at Queens College, City University of New York where he gained a bachelor in computer science. He began buying art in diverse fields while in the city. As he was the first in a market with a scarcity of buyers and having acquired a deep knowledge in each field, he was able to snap up the best objects.

His philanthropic work included the endowment of Chairs in Islamic art at his alma mater, Queen's College in New York, and at the School of Oriental and African Studies (SOAS) in London, where he was awarded his PhD. He also endowed the Khalili Research Centre for the Art and Material Culture of the Middle East at Oxford University.

In 1978, he moved to London after meeting his wife, Marion, who was working in an antiques centre and it was love at first sight. His real estate ventures include many major commercial and residential properties in the UK. In the early 1990s, he bought 18 and 19 Kensington Palace Gardens which were the former Russian and Egyptian embassies. Then he embarked on a renovation programme to change the buildings into a palatial equivalent to the White House and he imported the same inlaid and carved marble from the Agra quarry that was used on the Taj Mahal. As the most expensive house in the world at the time, it was later sold to the Indian steel magnate Lakshmi Mittal. Another important acquisition and redevelopment project was Bath House on Holborn Viaduct, which became the UK HQ of Amazon.

"I'm very democratic towards my family that consists of my wife Marion, our three sons, Daniel, Benjamin and Raphael," he said. "Whenever you are in a crowd and do not know where to go, put a child on your shoulder and they will tell you where to go."

All along he has had a spiritual approach towards art and life. He is insistent that his collections belong to humanity and if there is any praise it is not for him but rather for the souls

The Khalili Collections' Japanese three-piece garniture.

of the artists who produced such magnificent work.

"Ownership is a myth; we are only temporary custodians of what we think we own," he insisted. "My mission is to share the art with humanity – which is why I am one of the most active UNESCO Goodwill Ambassadors."

This attitude has also been recognised by the Catholic church. As a result he has received knighthoods from two Popes. Pope John Paul II honoured him as Knight of the Pontifical Equestrian Order of St Sylvester (KSS) and Pope Benedict XVI further elevated him to Knight Commander in the said order (KCSS) for his work in the pursuit of peace, education and culture amongst nations. In fact when Pope Benedict XVI awarded him with the honour, he said Khalili had the combined wisdom of three religious leaders: a chief rabbi, a cardinal and a grand mufti. And yet he remains incredibly humble: "Glory belongs to God and humility belongs to man," he said.

"My philosophy is the same as Maimonides," he continued. "It's the need to learn about other people's ways of life. By learning about it we will find there is more that unites us as human beings than divides us. We must move beyond mere 'tolerance' and learn to respect each other's world views."

It is not surprising, therefore, that

his Foundation has been at the forefront of interfaith dialogue for over three decades, and that one of the key projects – the Maimonides Interfaith Initiative – has been focused on interfaith cohesion through art, culture and education. His powerful partnership with the Commonwealth (Faith in the Commonwealth) has facilitated grassroots peace activism that has reached some 16,000 youth in countries across Africa, South Asia and the Caribbean.

The list of honours he has received is substantial, but to name a few he is Trustee of the City of Jerusalem, a recipient of the High Sheriff of Greater London Award and is an Honorary Board Member for the INTERPOL Foundation for a Safer World (2018-2019). He has also received the rank of Officier in the National Order of the Legion of Honour by the French

President François Hollande at the Elysée Palace, who said of Khalili on the occasion that "he is a man who works for peace."

The number of serious collectors can be counted on one hand, such as the David Collection in Copenhagen, Sheikh Nasser al-Sabah of Kuwait, Chester Beatty and the Rockefellers. But some experts deem that it's the sheer depth as well as breadth of Khalili's art holdings which rivals that of the Getty or the Gulbenkian.

In fact Susan Moore, of the Financial Times and Apollo Magazine, placed him in a class of his own: "David Khalili puts most collectors to shame," she said. "In an age in which many rich men call themselves collectors and seem more interested in displaying their wealth than the art they have acquired through it, Khalili has done rather more than simply raise a paddle in the sale room."

"My hunt for objects is adventurous," he said. "I once was in restaurant in the US and I spotted a Japanese enamel vase that I recognised as being the missing piece of a huge eight foot tall 3-piece garniture made specially for the World's Columbian Exposition in Chicago in 1893, which attracted 27 million visitors."

Dubbed at the time 'the largest examples of cloisonné enamel ever made' the garniture took five years to complete and was commissioned by Shin Shinwoda, the Special Councillor for Arts of the Imperial Commission to the Exposition. The manufactures were Shirozayemon Suzuki of Yokohama and Seizayemon Tsunekawa of Nagoya. The greatest imperial court artists of the period were employed in their creation – with an all-star team of the most celebrated artists including Araki Kampo (1831-1915) and Oda Kyōsai (1845-1912) overseeing the designs. Upon completion, the Emperor of Japan had subsequently reviewed them ahead of the exposition.

"The vase I'd spotted in the restaurant

was purchased in Chicago by Frank Spenger," he continued, "and brought to the California Midwinter International Exposition of 1894, which explains how it eventually made itself to Berkeley, California. Finally, in February 2019, I purchased the last missing vase from an auction house in Auckland, California."

After over 120 years of separation, the famous three-piece garniture had finally been reunited in Khalili's Japanese Art of the Meiji Period (1868-1912), finding their rightful place in what is considered, alongside the Japanese Imperial Collection, to be the world's most significant collection of its kind.

This marked the latest achievement in a long history of separated artworks (originally belonging together as a unit or a pair) being reunited by David Khalili. His remarkable stories of acquisition are endless.

"One of my most notable acquisitions is a written history of the world by Rashid al-Din from the 14th century, commissioned by a Mongolian khan, "he said. "I bought it for a fortune in 1990 from a collector who had bought it at a Sotheby's auction ten years earlier. It is called Jami' al-Tawarikh or Compendium of Chronicles, which includes the earliest purely landscape miniature of any known manuscript and today is considered priceless."

David Khalili is a household name within the areas that he collects in, and is particularly well regarded among the elite of the art world. But unlike many other billionaire collectors he doesn't buy for self-indulgence or monetary gain. His aim has always been to reach out and share these treasures with others as his motivations are humanistic and educational. Selected objects from his collections have been shown in several major museums and been displayed as part of international exhibitions such as the British Museum, the Victoria and Albert Museum and Somerset House (London); the State Hermitage Museum (St Petersburg); the Alhambra Palace (Granada); the Metropolitan Museum of Art (New York); Portland Art Museum (Oregon, US); and the Van Gogh Museum (Amsterdam) among others. In fact, his collections have been the subject of over 120 exhibitions worldwide that have been visited by an estimated 20 million people so far.

David Khalili views philanthropy differently to other philanthropists. For him, collecting must itself be an act of cultural philanthropy, whereby the true collector fulfils five essential criteria: collect, conserve, research, publish and exhibit. What's more, he has now added 'digitization' to this robust criteria, and his partnership with Google – which is designed to use cutting-edge technologies to optimise viewer experience online – shows that he is ahead of the times, as he always seems to have been.

Muse of Classical Music

Mrs Aline Foriel-Destezet's contribution to the music world is immeasurable. She has made the classical music world a richer place through her selfless devotion to new talent and making high quality performances feasible through her donations. I cannot think of any other person who has done so much.

It not unusual to find that Aline spends four to five days of her week shuttling between performances at opera houses such as La Scala, Paris, the Centre of Baroque Music in Versailles as well the concerts in Chantilly castle. She is a maecenas at the festivals of Lucerne, Verbier and the chateau de la Moutte in St Tropez, among others. She also gave a concert in the Victoria Hall in Geneva as well as the Camerata Geneva and operas in the Grand Theatre, Geneva.

"In London, I am the maecenas of Royal Philharmonic Orchestra, Covent Garden," said Aline who radiates vitality and is full of youthful energy. "In a few days I'll be in Zurich to listen to Martha Argerich with the conductor Charles Dutoit. I also support the foundation of the Children of Peru concerts and meet with musicians. And I enjoy every minute of it!"

The three musical events in Gstaad - Menuhin Festival, New Year Music Festival and the Sommets Musicaux, have been enhanced and benefitted greatly by her interest and active support. But above all, she participates in the design of the scenery for operas and Carmen was the latest success at the Menuhin Festival. She also provides advice to artists such as Joyce Dent and Gustavo Dudamel.

"Ten years ago the Menuhin Festival Menuhin wasn't important and I wanted to build it so I asked new artists," said Aline whose brown eyes sparkle as she talks. "One of the highlights was Sir Antonio Pappano, the Russian singer Valerie Gagreff and the exciting performances by opera singer Diana Damrau, Juan Diego Flórez and Jonas Kaufman. I love Anna Netrebko and Sonya Yoncheva whom I heard in Geneva. It's impossible to name all the artists. But my most exciting discovery was the violinist Daniel Losakovitch whom I found as a boy in Vienna."

Her interest in classical music all started when Aline was eight and was taken to see Puccini's powerful masterpiece, Tosca. It was an unforgettable experience as it was sung by Maria Callas who for her was the greatest soprano. She heard Callas both in Norman and Tosca under the baton of Arturo Toscanini. As a girl her passion was to become a ballet dancer but her family suggested that it would be better if she studied something and attended music and ballet performances for pleasure. She studied art at the Louvre and philosophy at the Sorbonne.

"I am my happiest when I listen to music," she said. "And my favourite composer is Wagner. I've heard performances at Covent Garden, Munich Opera House and Salzburg Festival and I've found that besides exceptions like Bryn Terfel, German singers are the best because the lyrics are in their mother tongue."

Silence is Also Music

She was born in Jallieu near Lyon, France and as her father's family always had classical singers around, she was familiar with such an ambiance. Aline married young and had four children. Her husband is the French billionaire Philippe Foriel-Destezet who founded Adecco, the recruitment agency. She has lived with her husband in the UK for some 22 years.

"When it comes to opera houses, I can name my three favourites," she said. "Covent Garden is the first on my list because among other things its perfect acoustics and excellent organisation. The second is Paris and the third is La Scala in Milan. But there are times when I shutoff from music and go on my boat sailing on the sea. I like to be on the boat with nobody. It's a pleasure. There is no music but the silence is also music. I'm away for about ten days and spend the time reading philosophy."

Aline is in her element too when she talks about musicians like the young violinist Daniel Losakavich whom she met when he was eight. "My most important task is to help musicians," said Aline. "I have five assistants just for that purpose."

What a charismatic woman! She can solve life's problems just by reading a passage in a philosophic work or by being elevated to a happy state through music.

Royalty Galore

HRH Prince Michel of Yugoslavia is an investment executive, a polyglot, a socialite, a philanthropist and a talented photographer. He grew up in Versailles but always had ties with Gstaad as a child and later as regular skier at the resort. He was sent as a boy (9-11) to Marie José boarding school which was named after his grandmother who was the daughter of the King of Belgium. It was a tough environment as the pupils had to walk up the steep slope in winter to Wassergrat to ski. After his baccalaureate, he gained an MBA from the European Business School, Paris.

"My venture into photography happened by chance," he said. "A friend, Giovanni Rondanini, knew about my photos and invited me to join four Italian artists in a exhibition. To my surprise I sold 30 photos compared to the few sales of the prominent artists. It was incredible because I had no idea of what size to make the photos nor of how to print them. My girlfriend who lived in Belgrade saved the day by printing them and sending them by bus in a cardboard tube. I mounted them in frames and cleaned the glass with window cleaner."

Prince Michel started in a brokerage firm before he joined Sotheby's

HRH Prince Michel of Yugoslavia

International Realty in Palm Beach (1985-1999). A memorable moment in his life was his first sale in Florida of the most expensive mansion in the city. It was the easiest as a couple who were put off by a brash colleague asked him to handle the transaction. His next position was in a marketing company, Access group, New York. (1999-2008) which was followed by being appointed as a senior advisor to Diligence Global Business Intelligence (2010-2017).

Golden Greeks

"During the financial crisis I consulted my goals coach, Nicole Petschek, who suggested that I start a new career," he said. "But she also advised me to pick a hobby. It was great insight as I already had a good eye for art and beauty through visits to museums, art fairs and galleries. In addition, I'd lived in Versailles which gave me an understanding of the golden proportion according to the Greeks. This prepared me for a career in art photography."

Michal, along with his twin brother, Dimitri, are the eldest sons of Prince Alexander of Yugoslavia and his wife Princess Maria Pia of Savoy. Through his parents he is related to every royal family in Europe, making him over 1000th in the line of succession to the British throne. He also has ancestors with artistic traits such as Prince Nicholas of Greece and Denmark and the Grand Duke Vladimir of Russia.

His maternal grandmother was Princess Marie Jose of Belgium, whose father was Albert I, King of the Belgians. His paternal grandmother was Princess Olga of Greece & Denmark (sister of Princess Marina, Duchess of Kent). His paternal great grandfather was Prince Nicholas of Greece & Denmark, an avid oil painter and son of George I (1845–1913), King of the Hellenes. His paternal great great grandfather was the Grand Duke Vladimir of Russia, patron of the avant-garde, who inspired the creation of the Ballets Russes.

Closing a Deal is Fun

Antonia Crespi Bennassar is the queen of real estate in Gstaad. It is quite an achievement because the clientele is very demanding and very few of the wealthy owners of exclusive chalets come to the market. How she, who was born in Majorca has come to be a power woman in the resort is an interesting story. One of the compliments she received was from Christian Völkers CEO of Engel & Völkers AG. "Crespí has been the company's most successful real estate consultant for many years," he said.

"The appeal of the resort to the most sophisticated and wealthy is a combination of factors," said Antonia Crespi, a charming and attractive woman. "The fantastic landscape, the restrictive building regulations, the infrastructure and the fact that one can relax undisturbed in the place. On my side as a real estate entrepreneur, it's about working hard, building trust

Antonia Crespi Bennassar

and understanding the lifestyle of the clientele."

Her defining moment was at Art Basel when she approached Christian Völkers. "Hi, you don't know me but I know you," she said because she had seen him around in Majorca. She told him that she had clients in Switzerland and wanted to move there. Her children were at J.F. Kennedy international school, Gstaad and she wanted to be with them. The next day, she was tracked down by Völkers' assistant who arranged a meeting. It resulted in her gaining a franchise of the Engle & Völkers company.

"I didn't know anyone in Gstaad and

nor was I a member of the jet set," she said. "It was daunting prospect as everyone wants to gain a foothold in this exclusive market. I started from scratch with no office, no connections and didn't know my way around the place. My first client was the CEO of a bank. His secretary contacted me about finding an apartment to rent and I later located a property for him. Then I had my big break when a client came to the office and wanted to buy a rustic farmhouse. I talked to many owners and made a deal for eight figures. That was over 10 years ago."

Antonia was born in Majorca where her family were landowners and had vineyards. Her father, Sebastian, was an entrepreneur and opened the first advertising agency. She studied art history and followed with a masters degree in contemporary art with Sotheby's. Then she joined her father in his business and learnt empathy and skills to understand the aspirations of customers. Before long, she started her own real estate agency. She had two children Sebastien Owen who is studying chartered accountancy and her daughter Maria Elisabeth who graduated at St Martins College of Art.

Like Federer I don't Know How to Cheat

"My father was a creative, noble person who taught me to have a rapport with others and honesty if I wanted to network," she said. "Gradually, I built up a reputation in real estate and had clients with famous names who were generous in giving me their trust. Like Federer I don't know how to cheat. But I love to find solutions. And success is always about work, discipline and being there when the situation demands it. Also, I've always been determined and had positive attitude to life."

One of the highlights of her career was the promotion as head of the Private Office of Engle & Völkers in 2017. It provides an individually tailored service like temporary rental and dealing with yachts and aircraft for the ultra high net worth individuals of whom there are 2,000 to 3,000 worldwide. Her experience in discrete search mandates in Gstaad made her an ideal candidate for the post.

"I resigned after a year and a half because I preferred the cut and thrust of sales," she said with a smile. "What gives me most fun is closing a deal when it's 80 or 90% complete."

But like her clients she enjoys the landscape not just for its beauty but through physical activity. She is an avid hiker and after three or four hours of hard slog, the reward is a breathtaking view. For example, at the top of the Oldenhorn you can see the Bernese Alps, 24 summits over 4000m high such as the Mont Blanc and the Matterhorn.

"I love hiking in the mountains because it gives me a sense of belonging here and being part of the community," she said. "It also imparts an understanding of the landscape. I have little patience for yoga but I enjoy swimming during the low season, after all I come from the island Majorca."

Her other passion is art and a favourite artist is Joan Miró who was a simple man with a very routine life but creating poetical artwork. She also contributes to the community by sponsoring the tennis, the Menuhin Festival, the Country Night, among others In 2018, she co-founded a gallery space, Tarmak 22, at Gstaad airport with Tatiana de Pahlen, the Agnelli heiress and is a member of the new Club de Luge. The exhibitions have included collaborations with the Gagosian gallery and Alex Hank private collection.

Antonia is one of a kind. Spanish by birth, brought up by the sea and yet now totally at home among mountains in a German Swiss canton. She is an independent woman, inspired by the American artist Louise Bourgeois and yet modest. Without doubt, she is a role model for girls in the 21st century.

How Three Months Became 35 Years

Robert Speth is one of the great Swiss chefs and has been the culinary king of Gstaad for over 35 years. He is known for big cuts - he would never use tweezers in his cooking, and his warm geniality towards his clients. He and wife Susanne who ensures that everything runs smoothly and the guests are happy, always had time to relax with a glass of wine or on the golf course. A three month engagement in 1984 as a chef from Germany to help a friend led to a new life in Switzerland.

"Those three decades at the Chesery have been one long holiday," he said with a smile, "because I consider cooking as a form of pleasure and not work. A lot has changed in that period because when I first came to the Chesery which was owned by the Aga Khan, celebrities held parties in the restaurant. Now they entertain in their chalets."

Robert Speth's father was a farmer from lake Constance. He completed apprenticeships as a pastry chef and a cook. Later, he worked with top chefs in La Napoule and Munich before being appointed head of the party service department at the Steigenberger Hotel Frankfurter Hof in Frankfurt.

Hooves on Cobblestones While You Eat

"My special requests from clients have varied from cooking lamb covered in grass in an earth oven for nine hours," he said, "or turning alpine pigs on a spit in the mountains. Once a reservation was made at 11pm for a Saudi prince for 60. He wanted three of everything - appetisers and starters, a lamb and a fish. We waited for him and his entourage until 5am and eventually three people turned up! We also arranged horses to pass by during a meal as the prince was so fond of hooves on the cobblestones."
He has excited the palates with

Robert Bratschi and Robert Speth

his three flavours per dish, his masterpieces like sea bass in a salted crust, egg brûlée topped by caviar and the legendary truffle brie. His insistence on fresh products means that some never see the inside of a fridge like mushrooms or alpine strawberries which arrive in the afternoon and are served in the evening. His insistence too of seeing the meat on the bone and choosing choice cuts from the carcass. But above all, his main concern was please his customers and while doing so, received accolades from Michelin and Gault Millau.

The inhabitants of Gstaad salute you - the clients including 2nd and 3rd generations, fellow golfers and suppliers like Robert Braatchi and Walter Schmidt. You have served everyone with distinction. But we are glad that you will still be around offering special catering.He can be contacted at:

Le Grand Catering
Tel. 079 748 0123
catering@bellevue-gstaad.ch.

Mehran Azmoudeh

Mehran Azmoudeh is one of the exceptional students that graduated from the prestigious boarding school Le Rosey. He is a gifted mathematician who studied applied mathematics at the University of California, Berkeley and gained a Masters at Imperial College, London.

Mehran Azmoudeh

He started his own software company in Silicon Valley, then became an oil and gas consultant and finally founded a private equity company. But he also has a global platform as the president of Le Rosey's Alumni association aka Association Internationale des Anciens Roséens (AIAR).

"My father, Manucher, who's in the oil and gas industry was disappointed when I didn't join him," he said with a broad smile, "After two years, I returned to London and set up an oil consulting company. But I opted for a different name, Jack Harper, and not my own. It led to one of my proudest moments in my life. My first agreement was with a Russian company for offshore drilling in the Persian Gulf. I had to go to Moscow so I sent Jack Harper off to Africa and Mehran Azmoudeh went to Moscow. I stayed at the Metropole which was then the top hotel and visited Red square.

Mehran first came to Switzerland at the ages of six and seven when he attended summer camps in Crans Montana. He was scheduled to return to Iran in 1978 when the revolution started and he had a choice of schools in the UK or Switzerland. He decided on the basis of which institution didn't require a school uniform and that's how he went to Le Rosey aged eight. There were a lot of Iranians there and was an amazing experience. It gave him a sense of security during the troubled times when his parents didn't have a place to settle down and make a new home. The fact that he was returning to his school, to the same people, the same rooms, and the same routines was an important constant in his life.

"When I was in the oil industry I had a near death experience," he said. "and was only saved by my lack of punctuality. We were in Iraq three months after the troops had entered the country. One morning, I got up late for my pickup to take me through a checkpoint in Baghdad. The woman driver was angry with me as she had scheduled the arrival 15 minutes earlier at 9am. We were at the back of the queue when we suddenly heard an explosion ahead of us and saw everything thrown up in the air. She turned round to me in the back seat and said,'Thank you very much.'"

Later, he joined his father and they had a lot of fun working together. They represented major oil and steel interests in the Middle East and Italy's biggest company, ILVA. For the past four years, he has run his own company Servonet Inc based in Palm Beach, Florida. He travels for his work while his children live in New York.

"This is my second mandate as president of AIAR," he said. "I built on the great work of my predecessor Evelyne Petten. I've brought an exceptional level of energy and ability to motivate younger members who are all volunteers. Consequently, the average age of the 5,000 anciens and anciennes is now 20 compared to 40 years in 2016. My job is to get people to give time specially those who don't have time. I exploit their love of the school to get time for participating in events and meetings."

Gstaad is the home of the AIAR and once a year in February a general assembly is held there. Over a 1,000 people attend from 70 countries in what is called the Rosey 'Long weekend.' It's an age-old school tradition that brings together Roseans, parents and the anciens who attend academic meetings and enjoy sporting and social events over three intense days.

8 Decades Link

Hans Ruedi Spillmann (HRS), has been associated with Gstaad for almost eight decades. His family arrived in the resort because his grandfather, an industrialist who had a pulp factory in Solothurn, bought a chalet in 1941 when he was four years old. His parents continued the tradition and so did Spillmann who bought the chalet Montesano, which was a former girls' school. Today, he lives in a chalet on the Wispile to accommodate his large family.

"My father was one of the founders of the Eagle Ski Club," he said. "How did it start? There was no snow in the early 1960s for St. Moritz while Gstaad had a lot. This attracted newcomers from St. Moritz, who suggested that something similar to the Corviglia club should be started in Gstaad. As my father and his pioneering friends built the first cableway station at the Wasserngrat in 1946, it was natural to site the Eagle Ski Club up there. Over the decades, the Club has become a second home to many of us." (See entry, Eagle Ski Club).

Spillmann studied law at Geneva university and after a banking career he finished with a partnership at Lombard Odier. He was the first Swiss German to join the bank and he was proud that he had the opportunity to work there. He has two sons who live in Geneva and London respectively, one of whom followed in his footsteps. They both have their own chalet in Gstaad.

Hans Ruedi Spillmann (HRS)

"Like my father before me, I was invited to join the Eagle Ski Club committee where I remained for a record of over 30 years," he said. "I collect Swiss art and have works by Cuno Amiet and Ernest Bieler, among others. The first artwork I bought from a dealer who had a problem distinguishing a fake from an authentic work. It was a painting by Fernand Leger and I liked the colour composition. Today I am still not sure if it is a fake of not. My wife, to whom I've been married for almost 60 years, collects drawings.

Spillmann is full of anecdotes. One of them is about the first tourists in the region. When the mountain railway (MOB) came, they were attracted to Château d'Oex, but the rich farmers whose Etivaz cheese had made them wealthy sent them to Gstaad. The reason was that the farmers in Gstaad were poor and needed the income from tourists.

Gstaad Photo Winner

Evelyne Peten

Gstaad is my home. I grew up here and my heart is here. My grand-parents started coming to Gstaad after the war for skiing holidays and stayed at the Palace. They then settled in Gruben and sent me first to Marie-José, a small boarding school for very young children and later on to Le Rosey. During my years at university in Boston and Brussels, where I studied clinical and experimental psychology, I always came back for my holidays, winter and summer. The attraction grew stronger. Driving from Brussels, there is a place on the road after Saanenmöser where the view opens up on to the Bernese Alps. It's a breath-taking sight which sends triggers to my brain: I'm home!

Photography has always been my hobby. It became a serious passion when I moved back to the Saanenland so that my daughter could go to the Kennedy School. At the same time I also discovered mountaineering with Ueli Hauswirth, a local mountain guide. Ueli has led me to the top of each one of our local peaks and far beyond, in all seasons, on foot and on skis. It has been over 20 years and I am forever indebted to him for having enabled me to fall in love with the mountains.

Evelyne Peten

When climbing to the top of these mountains, I am constantly awe-struck by their serene yet cataclysmic beauty and often stop to take pictures, much to the aggravation of my companions. Mountains are awe-inspiring to me. Orogenesis is also one of my interests which has resulted in thousands of photos of rocks that will hopefully be of significance to a geology professor. Probably posthumously alas!

I am currently finishing yet another degree in photography where I am to practice on subjects such as people, who tend to move quicker than rocks! I am also involved in various local associations, clubs and schools in the Saanenland.

It is my opinion that the best attitude to have in life is to be open-minded towards others, forgiving towards yourself, to always doubt and to have a serious sense of humour. Life's better when you're laughing!

She won the Gstaad Best Photo award selected by a distinguished panel of Irene Kung - one of the great fine art photographers, Patricia Low - a top galerist who has handled Gerhard Richter, Andy Warhol etc and Frank Müller - the publisher of Gstaad My Love and Gstaadlife among others. (See separate entries for all).

Writers' Haven

Vera Michalski-Hoffmann is a charismatic figure. She exudes a gentle charm, a tranquility that belies a deep spirituality and a clear-eyed honesty. Besides being a publisher, a patron, a member of numerous cultural associations around the world, she has two paradises in her life. The natural one where she has a chalet - Gstaad and the other which she created in Montricher - The Foundation for Writers and Literature.

"Although I learnt to ski in the Grisons, my fondest memories are skiing on the Wasserngrat at the Eagle Ski Club," she said. "Another is driving to Gsteig and taking the little cable car to the Sanetsch pass and skiing down into the Valais. There was a good choice of wine, raclette, fondue or rösti. At the ski school my daughters were terrified of a dragon teacher who didn't understand the psychology of children. They can be taught by having fun."

Vera leads a busy life in Gstaad as she is very community-minded. She has the reputation of taking all her commitments seriously as her conviction is that having money also confers responsibility. She is the president of Sommets Musicaux de Gstaad as well as being a member of its Honorary Committee. She supports Elevation 1049, the biennial art event which encourages young artistic talent. Another music festival, the Menuhin also receives her patronage.

"One of the reasons for buying the Chalet in Gstaad was that I didn't want my children to be boarders in Gstaad," she said. "They went to the local schools in Montricher and when they went to Le Rosey we bought the chalet. It was a good move because the children tended to be ill during winter along the lake. Up in Gstaad they were healthy during the winter term. As few parents were around in the winter, I became a surrogate mother to my children's friends. One of the delights of the village is the promenade because before the big brands took over, there were many local shops like the von Siebenthal kitchen store on three floors where you could find wonderful things. There was also a local cafe with a pub at the back where today there's the Cappuccino restaurant."

The other paradise is under lofty concrete columns that resemble trees and their foliage is at the foot of the Jura with stunning views onto Lake Geneva. Indeed the Foundation Jan Michalski for writing and literature is one of the important cultural foundations in Switzerland which Vera Michalski-Hoffmann established in 2009. Her vision was to create a concept of a haven for writers designed with a multitude of functional spaces "like a small city" devoted to writers and literature. But it's more like a modern version of Plato's Academy except the writer and not the philosopher is dominant.

If there is maxim which has driven her it's "The pen is mightier than the sword." It is the very motive that launched her and her late husband, Jan Michalski, on the path to publishing. The first book they published was written by a prisoner of the Soviets under Stalin, the Polish painter Josef Czapski and was titled, Proust against Defeat. He was imprisoned after the invasion of Poland in 1939 and lectured on Proust as an act of resistance against the barbarity of the camp. It served as a template for survival.

"Literature is the poor relation of culture," she said. "It's more difficult to get help when you are a young writer than if you curate a large exhibition on Gauguin. One of the interesting writers-in-residence in 2019 was Fatin Abbas who was born in the Sudan and has a legacy of slavery in her family. Another is Rana Dasgupta, an Indian from the UK educated at Oxford and a member of India's most prestigious literary award: the JCB Prize for Literature."

Eagle Ski Club

Loula Chandris is the first woman president of the prestigious Eagle Ski Club. She is eminently qualified and a natural successor of Urs Hodler as she spent 10 years on the committee and six years as Vice President. (See separate entry, Hodler). She was responsible together with Urs for the outstanding 50th jubilee celebrations in 2007. Her parents Aleko and Marietta were one of the first life members of the Eagle Ski Club.

"I spend my time between Greece and Gstaad," she said. "Both are exceptional places. Greece has a special light that inspires artists and Gstaad is a paradise. Once I said as much to my driver as we passed St Stephan on the way to Gstaad. 'Of course, its a paradise,' he replied,'God placed his hand on this area when he made the earth.' I was surprised by the explanation but it's truly beautiful."

"Gstaad and the Eagle Ski Club belong together," she said. "I first came to Gstaad when I was nine years old and attended the Marie-José. My parents bought a chalet and we loved the resort from the moment we arrived: the people, the beautiful village and seeing the same friendly faces every year. I also learnt to ski with Bethli Küng-Marmet, a former Swiss ski champion who taught the whole Goulandris family. (See separate entry, Bethli) At that time, I spent a large part of my life in Gstaad and enjoyed every moment."

Loula's father who was a prominent shipping magnate, was one of the founders of the N.J. Shipping group as well as being an astute contemporary art collector and philanthropist. He was inducted into the Greek Shipping Hall of Fame posthumously in 2018 in the very Megaron concert hall where he once sponsored concerts to raise the spirits of the Greek people during a period of depression and austerity. And he did it anonymously.

He was also responsible for the rebuilding of the famous battleship, the Giorgios Averoff, which fought in four wars. It was an initiative he followed very closely even in the last days of his life. Today, it's a museum ship and tours around Greece.

Battleship Fought in Four Wars

He did countless acts of support for the Cycladic islands, particularly the island of his birth, Andros where among other things, he rebuilt the Tourlitis lighthouse in memory of his daughter, Violanda, who predeceased him. He also boosted employment to 400 from 30 after his company's takeover of the Neorion shipyards on Syros. Above all, Aleko Goulandris could communicate as easily with royalty as with seamen on the company's ships, he was instrumental in creating an extended family culture at N.J.Goulandris. He was a great man. Such is the heritage that Aleko Goulandris has passed on to Loula and her children, Anthony and Marietta.

"I'm proud that all three generations of my family, including my younger sister, Alexandra, are members of the Eagle Ski Club," she said. "I became a member in 1978 and enjoyed sports such as tennis, waterskiing and skiing which was my passion. I was elected to the committee in 2000. Then I became the Vice President under Urs Hodler and it was during his presidency that we managed to keep the club on the top of the beautiful mountain. I'm lucky to have a great committee and wonderful staff like secretariat of Marianne and Tess and the maître d 'hôtel Sergio and his team. The committee consists of 12 members and each have specific responsibility like finances, club races, premises etc."

Loula attended Le Rosey where she gained her baccalaureate and then worked for her father. She married the scion of another illustrious Greek family, Michael D. Chandris, who runs a conglomerate with shipping, hotels, and real estate, among other interests. She helped with the interior design of her husband's passenger ships in Germany which were created in a traditional and modern style.

Michael Chandris paid tribute to his father-in-law at the Greek Shipping Hall of Fame. "Aleko was charismatic, self assured and clever," he said. "He always insisted on getting things done quickly and well. What I remember best of Aleko was his clarity of thought. He didn't say much but was analytical in the thought process. With razor sharp perception, he could understand a problem and he immediately found solutions. He had the ability to deliver and to create. His success in business was not just abut making money or more money than others, but to pursue his interests. He had a very good eye for art. From the 1950's and 1960s, he started buying art, what we now regard as modern art and it was a passion for the rest of his life. He applied the same decisive discipline to that as he did to his business and the same enthusiasm."

"Things have changed over the past decade at the Eagle Ski Club as members come and go more frequently," said Loula. "They don't stay for long periods as they did in the past. Now we have many more season and a few off-season members who come a lot during the low periods which is great as the Club is busy throughout the season. There is always a demand for membership as the children, grandchildren and even great grandchildren want to join. We are after all, a family club!"

Audrey Hepburn's Mother

Urs Hodler has shown a firm and committed leadership throughout his career. He was not only an officer in the Swiss mountain infantry for 2 years but when he was president of the Eagle Ski Club, he revitalised the Club and put it on a sound financial basis. In addition, he encouraged sports among the youth as well as competitions among international clubs. He also founded and headed the global investment group Octogone which was launched in Geneva.

"My first job was at J.P.Morgan in Zurich," he said. "Subsequently, I was promoted unit head of Morgan's Petroleum Department in New York. This was the hot spot in the 1970s where we syndicated large production payment loans for the major US oil companies such as Amoco Wallhalla in Norway and Mobil Arun in Indonesia. I'm proud to have had the opportunity of being part of such a prestigious bank."

He was born in Rome and educated at the ETH and University of Zurich. His father, Mario Hodler, worked for an Italian industrial and financial group and his mother, Lorna Baroness van Heemstra was a cousin of Audrey Hepburn's mother. For generations the van Heemstra family served the Dutch kings and queens directly and the kingdom as ambassadors.

Urs met his wife, Alice, at J.P.Morgan in New York. She subsequently became Vice President of Sotheby's USA. They have two children who are following in their parent's footsteps. Nicholas who gained a BA from Harvard and an MBA

Urs Hodler

from Columbia is now the Group CEO of Arc International, a multinational and the largest glass tableware company. Nicholas was twice the Swiss rowing champion in single and double sculling and with his Harvard team won the rowing championship against Oxford at Henley. His sister Carolyn holds a master's in art history and worked for Christie's as the head of the day sale in the Post-War and Contemporary department in London. She is a co-founder of the luxury evening wear and bridal collection company, Galvan London.

"My love for Gstaad began when my parents first rented a chalet and then built a chalet on the Grubenstrasse in 1974," he said. "When I became a member of the Eagle Ski Club in 1987, my children began to race and instead of just watching them, I joined them. I was appointed president of Sports and was successful in increasing the race participation of all ages by reaching out to the children who then drew their parents to the races."

The Eagle Ski Club organises eight Club races in winter and the cups are sponsored by members. In addition, the Eagle hosts two Interclub races, one for the teams of the Rosey, J.F. Kennedy schools and Eagle children. Urs replaced the 30-year-old Triangular Race between the Corviglia Ski Club of St. Moritz, Sci Club 18 of Cortina and the Eagle by the Eagle Winter Games for teams of distinguished clubs from Rome, New York, the Hague, London, Paris and South America. In addition, the Taki and Jones Trophies are awarded to the fastest winter and summer climbs up to the clubhouse.

"In 1998, there was a crisis of the Wasserngrat chairlift as the Swiss Department of Transportation decided to withdraw the operating concession of the then obsolete lift," he said. "The company did not have any funds for a new lift and the chairlift was the lifeline of the Eagle. It was the only means of reaching the clubhouse which is perched on rocks at an altitude of 2,000m. Over CHF 10 million were needed to build a new lift and snowmaking machines."

Under the tenure of Count Edouard Decazes, the third Eagle President and Claude Barbey his Vice President, together with the other members of the Committee, Urs succeeded in raising funds from the membership and built the new chairlift. Prince Nicholas Romanov succeeded Count Edouard Decazes as the fourth President and chose Urs as his Vice President. After six years, he was elected president, a position that he held for 10 years.

"I'm pleased because under my watch the Eagle achieved financial stability," he said. "The operating revenues now cover the operating expenses, new admission fees go to the capital account that among other things subsidises the lift. Passive members now pay an annual fee, membership rules are strictly enforced, the Club is also open in August and now has a competitive ski racing program. All this would have not been possible without the loyal support of my Vice President, Loula Chandris who succeeded me and the teamwork of the other eight members of my Committee. Life Members are proud of the achievements of Cedric Notz, one of our young skiers, who qualified for the Azerbaijan Olympic skiing team and went to Vancouver for the winter Olympics. The Tarantelli brothers, Leone and Uberto, are another example of young skiers who now race for the British ski team."

"My philosophy is simple," he said. "Whatever I do, I always give my best regardless of importance or resistance. My family motto is Fide virtute que famam quere. I told my children: 'you can always manage.' When they were growing up, we restricted television and gave them time without organised activities. Boredom itself is not important but what you do with it, is. We encouraged them to develop their creativity and discover their potential."

Maggots in Meat

"When I was a teenager at my grandfather's," he continued, "I was left on my own in his big property and I created my dream world of a hunter/gatherer. I built my own bow and arrows and was keen on fishing. I remember stealing meat from the kitchen which I would leave exposed for two weeks or more and produced maggots for my fishing hook. I spent hours observing and appreciating the causes and effects of nature. I think today's parents face an enormous challenge with the growth of virtual reality and social media that are creating a hyperactive but passive society."

Azerbaijan Olympian

Cedric Notz is the CEO and founder of FLOAT lending AG in Stockholm and an Olympian. FLOAT is the first digital-platform where small to medium-sized companies (SMEs) can receive fast, easy access to founder-friendly, non-dilutive growth capital. Above all, he is a cosmopolitan who has lived in five countries: US (New York, Boston), Russian Federation (Moscow), Azerbaijan (Baku), UK (London) and Sweden.

"After the financial crisis and the strict regulations introduced by governments," he said, "banks accommodated multinationals like Volvo but SMEs were left on the sidelines. So I created a niche market for them. We combined the power of algorithms and human intuition to bring augmented intelligence that transforms the borrower's experience to indicate future income of these companies."

Cedric was born in Gstaad and educated at the J.F. Kennedy International School and at Aiglon college. Later, he gained a bachelor in ScienceFinance at Boston College (1993-1997). His first job was at Citi Group (1999-2002) where he worked in institutional sales for alternate investments. Subsequently, he was a manager for Hyperion Capital (2002-2005), co-founder AG Leasing (2004-present), consultant for Pequot (2005-2007), marketing for Noster Capital LLP (2011-2013), director of the EDL Capital board (2017- present).

"In 2007-2010, I took time off from my business interests to train for the Olympics," he said. "As a boy I was a keen skier like my parents and we all won trophies at the Eagle Ski Club. (See separate entries, Urs Hodler and Eagle Ski Club) My father lived through me and pushed me as skier. At the age of 11, I came 5th in the Swiss championships for the Junior Olympics.

Cedric Notz, wife Andrea Brodin and family.

Later, my father encouraged me to take time off from my business interests to compete for the Azerbaijan ski team. I was selected for the giant slalom and special slalom to represent them at the Vancouver Olympics. (2007-2010).

"My father came to Gstaad in the 1950s and he was more of an artist than a businessman as he had a passion for aesthetics," he said. "He was the first person to use old wood inside and outside the chalet. He was assisted by a farmer and builder Jakob Matti who would come to meetings with straw on his clothes.(See separate entry, Chaletbau Matti)."

Boy Pilot

Cedric is the son of two remarkable parents, Peter Notz, the Steel magnet and Brigitte Notz former super model and top skier. (See separate entry, Brigitte Notz.) He remembered how cool his father was when he told him he wanted to fly a plane. He was 15 at the time and they were driving past the East Hamptons. Peter Notz turned around the car and drove to the airport where he left his son with a pilot instructor. Cedric soon had his license and was flying Pipers and Cessnas.

"Wealth should not be judged in a materialistic manner," he said, "rather it should be measured by the accumulation of experiences. Life goes fast and you should enjoy and maximise it because it's over before you know."

Cedric is married to Andrea Brodin, a Swedish interior designer whom he met at the wedding of his best friend, Chris O'Neill, who married Princess Madeleine of Sweden.

Skiing Like Eagles

Bernard Nicod is a phenomenon or he even might be described as a force of nature. He sits in his office, this king of real estate who is # 1 in French-speaking Switzerland and whose domain stretches all along Lake Geneva. On his huge desk there are towers of files that relate to thousands of projects on construction, sales and rentals worth many billions since the agency's foundation in 1977. Yet this man for whom a computer is an anathema can locate a file almost immediately. Within seconds he finds one that refers to his membership of the Eagle Ski Club in 1984 and flourishes the copy of the two signed signatures, a friend of Ted Kennedy's and the Aga Khan that validates it.

"It's fun to think that as a student at the Abbey St. Maurice, Valais, I once skied on the Wasserngrat and entered the Eagle which looked so splendid," he said full of smiles and laughing, "and asked how much it cost to join, only to be told by Count Edouard Decazes that you need a good education to come in here. Then for eight years in a row I was in the winning ski team together with Franz Wehren, Giorgio Capodilista and Beat Walpoth. It was great being a member as I enjoyed sport and found friendship."

To give him credit, he was budding entrepreneur at St. Maurice selling button-down Oxford shirts and Italian moccasin shoes to his classmates. By the time he started his economic studies at Lausanne university, he had CHF 200,000 in the bank. He was one of the 15 students who had a car - Alpha Romeo spider sports car. But before he began, he had to do his military service. There he learnt about tenir - to hold your position and never give up. It was an experience that shaped his life. Not bad for a boy who was a black sheep of his family as he was the only member of his family from his grandfather down who never went into the medical profession.

"My proudest moment at the Eagle was when Prince Nicholas Romanov who was the fourth president appointed me to be the Finance and Construction member on the committee," he said. "He was one of my mentors and liked to talk about Russian history. His great great grandfather was Emperor Nicholas I, Tsar of all Russia and his grandfather was Grand Duke Alexei Alexandrovich of Russia, the General admiral of the Russian navy. Unfortunately, the Grand Duke Alexei was defeated during the war and relieved of his command. We laughed at his critics' description of his

Bernard Nicod and Ndeye Magniez Ciss

life as consisting of 'fast women and slow ships.'

But the most dramatic event was when the Romanovs were rescued in Yalta by the cruiser HMS Marlborough sent by King George V in April 1919.

Caressed His Feet

Nicod who is based in Lausanne lives in chalet Valerie in Gstaad and his neighbours are Mirjam Sachs and Bernard Picasso. He is involved in other activities in Gstaad such as the Vice-President of the Polo Gold Cup Gstaad, the Yacht Club and on the council of Wasserngrat 2000 AG. During the 25 years he has been in Gstaad, he has seen changes. When he first came in 1980s, there were the real rich and select families. Nowadays they come from everywhere and tend to be flashy.

"Prince Nicholas Romanov visited Russia for the first time in June 1992 and often gave talks about the Romanovs," he said. "On one such an occasion in Lausanne an old Russian woman came and caressed his feet. Afterwards, she gave him a pair of hand knitted socks to keep his feet warm. I confess that I cried when he died. Another of my mentors was Juan Antonio Samaranch, the dynamic IOC president who dazzled me and for whom I was a business advisor. I have framed pictures of both in my office."

Nicod's remarkable career began when he was a boy at the construction site of the family's new lakeside villa. It was a memorable experience as he was fascinated by the architect who had workers moving around on his orders. Today, he has 248 staff and 1,300 workers on the payroll. He still enjoys seeing a building constructed and it only becomes alive when people are living in it.

Shooting Monuments

Irene Kung is one of the great fine art photographers who lives in the Swiss village of Saanenmöser. She is a globetrotter and when she trundles her wheelie across the pebbles from her chalet-cum-studio to the station, she always feels a thrill. She may be heading for Beijing but when a villager asks the destination - she answers Zurich not to appear too grand. She feels the same emotion when she returns from a journey. It's always good to come home. After all, when she was a girl and the family walked up the Gstaad valley and came to Saanenmöser, her father exclaimed, "Wow, it's so open here and one day I would like to build a chalet here." And he did and that's where she lives today.

"My starting point as a photographer was to shoot monuments in Rome," said Irene, an attractive woman with an open smile. "When the gallerist, Valentina Bonomo, who was interested in my work heard about my subject, she disagreed because that was what everyone did in Rome. But I was convinced a 100% that it was the right decision. So I slept on it and the next morning invited her over to my studio to show her a print. Valentina walked into my studio saw my image at a distance and when she came nearer she was bowled over by the Pantheon image. That was my first photographic exhibition in 2007."

But Irene had found her metier as a painter years before in Rome when she worked as a gopher for a Roman artist. He also taught her to paint and she achieved early success as a gifted artist known principally for her still life painting. Her technique, modelled on Etruscan, Roman and Renaissance frescoes delicately described the tension between classical civilisation and the contemporary world. In all, she spent almost 30 years in Rome and left in 2013 for Milan. But after three years, she knew she had to go even further north, to the Saanenland, where something she couldn't describe, had called her home.

Irene was born in Bern. Her father was a businessman and her mother a Canadian painter. One of her fondest memories was of returning home after school into a quiet house and tiptoeing to find her mother next to a window painting. Later, she was sent to the same school as her mother in the south of France. Then with two girlfriends, she went off to Spain to learn the language. One of them, Jacqueline, who had studied art was her guide on her visits to the Prado.

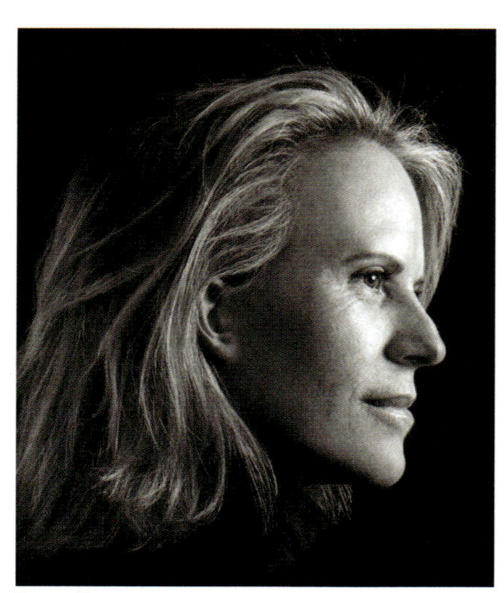

Irene Kung

"I was introduced to Velazquez there and later at the age of 20 to Picasso's Guernica," she said. "When I first saw the painting, I found it too abstract and only some 10 years later in New York did it make an impression. It hit me a lot because of the emotional suffering which I felt deeply. My inspiration comes from painters rather than photographers. I look at Caravaggio and Vermeer for light; Klee, Picasso and Richter for colour. When I walk around a city and take a photograph, I have a precise feeling of that moment. When I work in my studio, I try to bring that feeling back through my emotions. I don't think rationally but work intuitively, to get closer to the subject's mysterious and essential core."

Porsche Timeless Machine

She has achieved international recognition with exhibitions in New York, London, Milan and recently in Beijing and Moscow. She has exhibited at the Bozar Museum in Brussels, the Palazzo della Ragione in Milan and in the spectacular surroundings of the Certosa San Giacomo in Capri. She was invited by Contrasto to contribute to EXPO 2015 with a solo show at the Fruit and Legumes Cluster featuring 26 photographs of fruit trees. The most recent book Trees follows The Invisible City on architectural photographs.
In 2018, she created a collection of images for the launch of the Porsche 911. Limited editions are available from LUMAS.Com

"Sometimes, I'm asked what my philosophy of life is," she said. "It's to find the freedom of expression of one's emotions whether it's writing, painting or dance. So search for your personal truth and don't be put off by criticism. Be in touch with your intuition. My recent experience has been the Chinese culture. I've also found that whenever, there have been crises in their history, the artists have produced dreamlike work. But when things are back to normal, they produce realism."

Almost Killed in Avalanche

Brigitta Notz has been a glamorous figure in society for decades. She was a supermodel, a fashion designer, the third wife of steel baron Peter Notz and a local skiing champion. At the Notz's chalet, Les Anèmones, which was next to the Palace hotel, she was hostess to the A- listers in film, rock stars and fashion such as Roger Moore,

David Bowie, Roman Polanski, Curt Jurgens, Gunter Sachs, Joan Collins, Ivana Trump and Valentino.

"It was quite funny because people were queuing up to come to our chalet first and later went to the Palace and the Greengo nightclub," she said. "But that was when celebrities were one big family, all enjoying themselves. Nowadays, the super rich are all for themselves. Everybody is isolated, they don't communicate or have fun as we did. They call it being discrete! I remember a memorable occasion when David Niven, Peter Sellers and Roger Moore all competed against each other for the best jokes. It went on for ages and we were rolling on the floor. It's pity we didn't have iPhones then as we could've recorded the sessions. One of Roger's jokes was, 'what's the difference between the Eagle Ski Club and the sex position 69. At the Eagle, you see more old arseholes.'"

Brigitta was born in Graz, Austria and left home at 18 for Rome with CHF 50 and a couple of Italian words - grazie and spaghetti. A beautiful girl with looks like Heidi Klum and a body like Elle Macpherson she soon learnt another word, amore (love) through her boyfriend, Marquis Spinola. She was introduced to the high society and among others, met Princess, Irene Galizine, the Russian-Georgian fashion designer.

"My aim was to become a fashion model but when I applied at Valentino, I was shown the door," she said. "Irene Galizine gave me a start when I joined as a house model. Then I performed perfectly on the runway for a young Karl Lagerfeld, Emilio Pucci, Schubert, Givenchy, Fendi and Valentino where I became a principal model. One fashion moment which I will never forget occurred when I was wearing a red Valentino dress - a privilege given to a model at each show. When I looked in the mirrors, I could not hold back the tears because I appeared so beautiful. It was a see-through dress with big sequined roses later bought by Jackie O."

Brigitta was an instant celebrity, feted by the international media and was pursued by rich and powerful men including the Shah of Iran. She met Peter Notz, who was ultra charming, in the night club Greengo. They danced together that night and left at 6am and after three hours of sleep went on the slopes. Peter was one of the founders of the Eagle Ski Club and together with his friend Gunter Sachs they put Gstaad on the jet setter radar.

"I liked Peter from the start as we were on the same wavelength," she said. "I was impressed because he had three of the most beautiful homes I'd ever seen. We both enjoyed skiing and I began collecting trophies, winning all the Eagle Ski Club races in my category. One day, I was caught in an avalanche in the Diablerets and fell 200m. Luckily, the tip of my boot was visible. Peter was about

Brigitta Notz

to pull me out by the boot but the guide stopped him and said, 'we must free her face as her body is upwards.' He was right, I was choking. When I came down, one of the lift attendants recognised me as the woman in the avalanche. I wondered how he knew and when I looked at myself in a mirror, I realised why. I looked like a bloody monster! My face was swollen, nose bloody, violet rings under my eyes and blue lips.'"

Blowjobs

When her pregnancy prevented her from driving her Ferrari in comfort, she found an alternate means of transport. She gained a pilot's license for a Piper Aerostar plane at her husband's plane company, Aeroleasing. Gunter Sachs took stunning photos showing her incredible slim figure and her long legs when she launched her Pleasure Wear range of workout outfits for aerobics. One collector's item is a sexy back shot of her bending over and wearing her patterned leggings. Another presents her in turquoise leggings underneath a long white mink coat and a white fur hat by Aaron Slim.

"My son Cedric is in finance and was the best man to Chris O'Neal when he married Princess Madeleine of Sweden," she said. "Chris' mother and I are best friends and the boys grew up together. I'm proud of my daughter-in-law Andrea Brodin who is a star influencer in the social media as well as being a mother of three, interior decorator, home stylist, TV personality, author, presenter among other things. When it comes to advice to young men or women, I will be brutally frank. Men should get a career in social media and communication as banking is passé while women if they are pretty like some of the Russian girls should learn how to give a blow-job. The world will be open to them."

Brigitta Notz is a spunky woman who is high-spirited and courageous and still has her model figure. She is always on the go. One day she can be playing golf in Marakesh and next day skiing in Gstaad.

"I can't stand still for a minute and I do pilates, golf, skiing or hiking for three to four hours every day. My friends who have reached my age, sadly are unable to join me in sports or partying."

Compulsory 15 Minute View

David Koetser's idea of a busman's holiday is to spend four days with curators from The National Gallery, London exploring Florence. After all, it's still satisfying to study pictures in palazzos even after you've been in the art business for over 50 years. One could say it's in his DNA because both his grandparents were painters and his grandfather, Henri Koetser has 16 drawings and engravings in the Rjiks museum.

"I was fortunate when I was young because my father, Leonard, who had a gallery in London," he said, "made me spend two mornings a week with restorers and another two mornings at The National gallery. He insisted that I spend at least 15 minutes in front of each of three pictures. So began a good training for my future studies. The fifth morning could be spent in any gallery I chose.

"Today, I look at a picture for several hours if I'm interested. But I can also look at an old picture covered by dirt, varnish and several layers and would know what it would be when cleaned."

One of the highlights of his youth was when his father bought at auction the most expensive picture at the time - a Sir Peter Paul Rubens' Adoration of the

David Koetser

Magi from the Duke of Westminster. He was 12 and couldn't help being impressed because the acquisition created a worldwide media frenzy. The picture was huge and a wall had to be knocked down at Sotheby's to put it on exhibition before the sale. The Rubens reached a record of £275,000 in June 28, 1959 and a headline in the Observer asked "Would the painting boom last?" Today, the picture hangs in the chapel of Kings college, Cambridge.

Old Master's Sleuth

"I'm amused by the Observer headline," he said, "when you think of the recent purchase of the Leonardo for $450 million known to be not in perfect condition. In museums most people take only a few seconds to look at a picture but it takes a lifetime of study to tell the difference without a laboratory between a forgery and an original. My father had a cause celèbre with a Renaissance artist, Francesco Raibolini aka Francesco Francia and his Madonna and child. He bought it for a modest sum from the Lt-Col. Hon. Thomas G. Morgan Grenville and it coincided with a painting at the National Gallery presented by Dr Ludwig Mond. When placed side by side, it was proven by the scientific staff that my father had the original work, which of course he knew from knowledge and long experience."

Now David Koetser who has sold Old Master Paintings to museums and private collectors all over the world has himself made discoveries over the years.

"Many of our clients for Old Masters tend to give their paintings to museums as they are becoming rarer in the market and there are tax advantages," he said. "They can then enjoy the artworks during their lifetime and the public gets the benefit after their death."

What is soon apparent in David Koetser's company is his genuine love of art. He relishes the experiences such as initiating and contributing to a museum exhibition of Pieter Claesz (National Gallery Washington, Haarlem and Zurich) and co-curating and contributing to the Still lives of Adrian Coorte Exhibition (Washington and the Mauritshuis, The Hague) to celebrate the career of the outgoing director of the Mauritshuis, Netherlands. He even took over the director's office one day a week to complete the exhibition.

Another experience which he finds satisfying is to persuade clients to loan their pictures for an exhibition at a museum or gift them to a museum. He is the perfect example as his family has donated a collection of Old Masters through the Koetser Foundation to the Kunsthaus, Zurich. In addition, he is one of the eight founder members of TEFAF Maastricht (The European Fine Arts Fair).

Anyone who either likes Old Masters and wishes to know more or who are professional collectors, would benefit greatly by meeting David Koetser. His knowledge is legendary and his library - both books and magazines, is comprehensive. He has lived in the region for over 30 years.

Cows and Cambridge

Marcel Bach is a self-made man and a property magnate who makes things happen in the resort. He is particularly proud of the new 5-star hotel The Alpina Gstaad in Oberbort aka Beverly Hills section of Gstaad which he built with his partner Jean-Claude Mimran.

As the son of a farmer, he made deals from an early age like buying and selling cattle and as a ski teacher, he

Marcel Bach

was comfortable with multimillionaires on the slopes and could point out a mountain that his family owned.

"My grandfather, Armin Maurer, was a bank manager for the BEKB," he said with a smile, "and as I was a mischievous child, I touched the alarm when I visited him. It was fun to see him running from his office to stop it. One of the important things I did was to learn languages through traveling abroad. I spent two years in Cambridge for English and in Argentina I was taught Spanish."

"My family has been here forever," he said with a laugh as the first mention of the Bach family dates back to 1312, "and it's natural that I care for the environment. The architecture is an example of preserving the classical Simmental three-story style which Saanenland municipalities ensured through passing laws in the 1950s. Another concern is global warming as we are at a lower elevation than other "snow secure" resorts higher in the clouds, I had to do something about it. I again teamed up with Jean-Claude Mimran and Bernie Ecclestone to buy the rights to the glacier ski area next door which we rebranded Glacier 3000."

Alpine Garden of Eden

What visitors like in the resort is the quality of life. For the celebrities who live here it's like an Alpine garden of Eden. Many reside in Oberbort or Gruben, the Bel Air of Gstaad, where the chalets might look like farmhouses but have several storeys below containing swimming baths, gyms, art galleries, among other things.

"The attraction of Gstaad is the cultural and sports facilities, modern infrastructure which includes an airport for private aircraft, the short distances and nature" he said. "We have taken care of the region and avoided the excesses of places like Crans-Montana and St Moritz thanks to strict building regulations."

His advice to the young generation is to work hard, to be patient and above all, deliver quality in whatever work you do.

Dead Sea Scrolls

Dariane Pictet is one of the rare people one meets in a lifetime because she reaches deep into the psyche and can unveil unlived lives. But she is more because she is an actress, an art collector, an author and editor who lives in a renovated farmhouse outside the village of Rougemont with a commanding view of the mountains and valley.

Many people forget that they have a inner life and as an analyst she can reveal it to them. She is touched by mystery and metaphors of poetry with its longing and its exposure to suffering and the joy. The poetic imagery of Rumi, Rilke, Emily Dickinson and Mary Oliver, among others, appeals directly to the soul. It reconnects to the immediacy of the world, to a time when people looked up at the moon and the stars with wonder.

"I was born in Geneva and at the age of 14 knew that I would be a Jungian analyst when I was older," she said. "At the age of 18 I left for New York where I gained a degree in Comparative Religion at Columbia university. It was only much later at the age of 35 after I had attended drama school in Paris and worked as a poetry editor for the Literary Review in London that I made a crucial decision about my life. It was a crisis and I asked myself what's it all about? Then I looked at the hundreds of books on Jung and self-help. It was literally the writing on the wall and it was time for me to become an analyst. So I got a diploma from the C.G.Jung Institute, Zurich."

For the next 20 years, Dariane practiced and taught in London and spent her weekends at her home in Berkshire. Then she moved back to her roots in Switzerland. Besides her patients, she is a lecturer and supervisor for the International School of Analytical Psychology in Zurich (ISAPZurich) and the Guild of Analytical Psychologists (GAP) London.

She is widely travelled and in 2016 she went to Qumran where the Dead Sea scrolls were discovered and to visit the ruins of the early Essene community. It was surrounded by a landscape of sand and bone and reminded her of another visit to the Sahara where she had mused over the Desert Fathers.

"I felt myself expand over the parched earth, wondering about consciousness," she wrote in a pamphlet of a brilliant lecture, Silence and the desert, she gave at the Guild of the Pastoral Psychology. "I briefly imagined consciousness as a force that holds and binds the universe together. I saw a web of being, containing all, permeating everything, the very stuff of the universe, transcending time and space, the source of all poetry and imagery. The silence permeating this great dry land allowed me to rise above the concerns of the world."

The theme of her lecture was silence, headed by a quote from the lyrics of Simon and Garfunkels' Sounds of Silence, and incorporated the writings of the mystics, the sayings of the Desert Fathers, of Jesus as expressed in the gospel of Thomas and of Meister Eckhardt. But what impresses one about Dariane is that she doesn't just sit in ivory tower or analyst's chair but goes out and experiences the things she writes or talks about. There she is walking in the Sahara desert at sunset and musing on silence and of the men and women who lived in the Egyptian desert and were the forerunners of the Christian monastic communities. Or lying with her arms outstretched along the folds of a dune in the Sinai desert and feeling "a dizzying feeling

Dariane Pictet

that I could now die; it felt like both the beginning and the end of time and filled me with an experience of pure being."

Her conferences and workshops are multicultural events and include concerts, performances and movies. One of her guests was Nicholas Vreeland who is the abbot of a Tibetan Monastery in India and the son of Ambassador Frederick Vreeland and grandson of the famous fashion editor Diana Vreeland. He is also known as the monk with the camera - he raised funds for the monastery through his photographic exhibitions and spends half his time in India and the other half in New York at the Tibet Centre.

Drink Addiction

Dariane has an interesting take on drink addiction as she worked in a rehab in a London for three years. Most people turn to the Alcoholics Anonymous for help as they give a 12-step movement to put people on a cure. But can one understand the reason why it happens? Is it simply a weakness and what's its origin. By definition its a chronic, a progressive, potentially fatal disorder marked by excessive and usually compulsive drinking of alcohol leading to psychological and physical dependence. "When you grow up with alcoholic parents, or around someone narcissistic or with a mother that puts herself first," she said, "you'll learn at 2 or 3 years old that you have to serve the mother or father and that's how you get the brownie points, that's how you get recognition and have some kind of safety in the relationship. It's a relationship called co-dependence. When we look deeper behind, we see huge walls of resentment, raging anger and fury."

"Realising that you may be codependent," she continued, "can be an astonishing moment in your life, but really it also marks the start of a new adventure. In psychology, it amounts to a breakdown because they have been cut off from themselves. They react and say, But I don't know who I am. It's also a terribly painful point when you realise that you're just an adaptation to others and it wasn't coming from your core."

Jung's Red Book, which came out after 50 years being deposited in a Swiss bank vault, created quite a stir worldwide. Dariane gave a lecture at the Bodmer Library and Museum in Geneva when it was exhibited there, and the Palatinate room was so full people that some had to sit on the floor. So Jung is alive and well in Geneva!

New Zealand Romance

Toni von Grünigen who is the president of the Saanen municipality is the right man, in the right place, at the right time. He has eight years experience on the council and as a farmer is the quintessential representative of the area. When he was caught in the media frenzy over the arrest of Roman Polanski, a local resident, he dealt with it in a calm manner and dismissed it as a Federal and Cantonal matter. His attitude is one of discretion and respect for the privacy of celebrities and others.

"Gstaad has a village character unlike St. Moritz and Davos," said Toni von Grünigen who is a quiet and prudent man that weighs his words carefully. "Farming is needed for tourism to flourish in our valley. The diversity and the contrasts that you see here are impressive. We have an intact agriculture that works and is appreciated by tourism organisations and guests. Both profit from common offers such as carriage rides or the sale of regional products. The significance is not lost in the municipal council as I'm one of four members who comes

Toni von Grünigen

from agriculture. The presidency is a challenge the appeals to me and I want to help the Saanen community through my work."

70/30 Politics/Farming

From 1993 to 2004, he worked for different commissions at the municipality. It included committees of planning and infrastructure before being elected to the municipal council in 2004 and chairing the finance committee. In 2012, he resigned from his post of vice-president and chaired the communal assembly until 2016. Then in 2017, he was elected as president of the Saanen municipality. His aim is to be a politician rather than an administrator and to be in contact with locals as well as tourists. His other priorities include the development of tourism in Gstaad to be the strategic responsibility of the council and young people to be given greater responsibility for future projects.

"My ancestors who have lived here for some 400 years, have been dairy farmers," he said. "I've carried on the tradition in Turbach and even visited New Zealand to spend time on a large farm with a herd of 170 cows. It was an interesting experience. I found that there were no sheds for the animals which were kept outside. It was a fateful visit because I met my future wife, Barbara, there in a pub. She was Swiss from Spiez and we married seven years later. We have two sons. Today, I spend 70% of my time in politics and 30% on the farm where I have to hire an employee."

Over the next five years, von Grünigen has a budget of CHF 148 million which is to be invested in sustainable projects. Some 7,200 people live in the municipality and Gsteig and Lauenen which are also part of Saanenland bring the total up 9,000. The population rises to around 30,000 twice a year when tourists and visitors come in the summer and winter periods. Compared to Interlaken which has similar number of households, Saanen has double the amount to spend on each, CHF 21,800 vs. CHF 10, 900.

Roman Polanski My Friend

Andrew Braunsberg is a film producer with many films to his credit. His way into the industry was by chance. He wasn't a graduate of a film school but had a solid background in education at Le Rosey from 9 to 13 and then Gordonstoun where he finished his studies. .(See entry, Le Rosey).

The first gave him a love of Gstaad and taught him French and the second enabled him to take everything that life threw at him in his stride and lend a helpful hand to those around him. He was brought up in the UK as his parents fled Germany before the Second World War.

"I've been coming back to Gstaad ever since I was a boy and I still keep coming back for more than 60 years," said Andrew, an affable and engaging man. "It's a magical place and those who live here have a common appreciation of the area. There's a reservoir of amazing people from all over the world who love the place. Le Rosey was the magnet."

The schooling at Gordonstoun made a deep impression on him because of the honours system. Each student was expected to be honest and to be responsible for their own life. They were given a training book in which different tasks had to be carried out but it was up to them. "Plus est en Vous" - there is more in you than you know, was the mission statement of the founder Kurt Hahn.

"My career in film came about by chance," he said. "because I could speak French, a friend of mine, rang me up one day and asked if I could show a French director around London. That's how I met Roman Polanski who became a friend and later, I became his partner and producer in the film business. Something deep inside appealed to me about the process of making films like the nomadic existence and the relationships that develop during the shooting. It's an intense family you're part of for a year or more and then it disintegrates. For the next film, it's a new family."

Andrew and Gabriele Braunsberg

Andrew's first film was *Wonderwall* which starred Jane Birkin, Irene Handl, among others, and the soundtrack was composed by the Beatle George Harrison. The film was released at the Cannes Film Festival in 1968. It coincided with the student protests in Paris which spread to Cannes and the festival was closed down in solidarity with the protests. There was mass evacuation. Nice airport was closed but the British send a aircraft to pick up their nationals.

During his career Andrew made his reputation with three films: *The Tenant* (1976) in which Polanski both acted and directed and starred Isabelle Adjani, Melvyn Douglas and Shelley Winters; *Being There* (1979) which was directed by Hal Ashby and starred Peter Sellers, Shirley MacLaine and Welwyn Douglas; and *The Postman Rings Twice* (1981) Jack Nicholson, Jessica Lange and Anjelica Houston.

One-Legged Terrorist

"One of my memorable adventures in film occurred when I made *Crusoe* which we shot on the Seychelles," he said. "It had a low budget and one of the key elements was to have a sailing ship that needed to look like an 18th century schooner. We organised this in Mombasa with an ex-guards officer who also agreed to find a crew to sail it over 1,000 miles to the Seychelles. When the vessel didn't appear on the scheduled date, we worried as every day was costing us a lot of money and we didn't have radio contact with the schooner. Finally, the ship appeared and my associate who went on board came to me white-faced and told me that it was captained by a one-legged terrorist and his gang. They were demanding £100,000 ransom to release it otherwise they'd blow it up. So after seeking and not getting any help from the Seychelles Foreign Minister, I got onto Lloyd's of London with whom we'd insured the ship. They sent out a tough ex-SAS chap who negotiated with the terrorists. After some very tense negotiations, a ransom of £25,000 was paid and we finished the film."

When Gabriele met Andrew Braunsberg on the roof of their Soho apartment building, in New York, in July 1983, it was a coup de foudre. They have been together ever since.

They have two children, Jeremy who is a filmmaker, and Olivia who teaches in a Montessori kindergarten.

Gabriele was born in Vienna where she grew up and went to school. She enjoyed the cultural life of the city going to the theatre, the opera, and the concerts of the Vienna Philharmonic, reading authors such as Arthur Schnitzler, Stefan Zweig and Joseph Roth. As a teenager she started attending the famous balls which offer a nostalgic atmosphere of the former glory of the Austro-Hungarian empire when the Emperor Franz Joseph opened the dances in the Hofburg palace to everyone. It enabled the Viennese to copy the court customs which included a strict dress code.

"My father, Gustav, was a businessman and my mother, Kristine, a doctor," she said. "I studied business administration at Vienna University because I thought it was a good platform to launch a career. I first went to London and then had my own company for film PR in New York. Since Andrew and I got married, we have been working together on several film projects. After we moved to Vienna I started to also produce documentaries for Austrian television, and write screenplays."

Her advice to the young is to be open-minded, curious and learn as many languages as they can.

Archive Writer

Benz Hauswirth is the local historian who can trace his ancestors back to the first family member called Benedicht in 1434. Other information can be gathered from the family coat of arms which depicts a house. It's likely to be landhaus which was used as an inn for travellers as well as a place for social and official events. What is interesting is that innkeeping was not a private enterprise but was a privilege granted to a person of integrity by the commune.

"I grew up in Gstaad where my father was a farmer and cattle dealer," he said.

"I studied in Bern and later worked for the Saanen commune where I was manager of the construction and planning department (1992 - 2008). However, I've always been interested in history in particular, the evolution of the Saanen house from the Middle Ages to the 20th century."

His interest in history includes giving guided tours on Saanen and writing books including a historical guide to Saanen (Saanen ein historische Dorfführer) co-authored with his partner Brigitte Leuenberger-Jaggi. Both have been in charge of the old archives in Saanen commune since 1992.

Eye Gouging

Hauswirth's last book which was published by Müller Medien in 2017 gives the reader extraordinary insights into a time from the redemption, from tax dodgers to drills, eye gouging and the first advertising posters of the Hotel Palace. (See separate entry, Frank Müller). Rémy Best, who is the owner of the Saali House in Saanen wrote the preface. He gave three reasons for his involvement with the book: Firstly, the responsibility to remember as he and his wife, Verena, believe that a community without knowledge of their past has trouble shaping their future. Secondly, the story of Saanenland with its 800- year old history where people have been innkeepers since 1312 and the women have been equal to their husbands for just as long in agriculture and thus had a pioneering role. And thirdly, the love for this beautiful area.

Hauswirth also has a holiday house in the Lauenen. It's a farmhouse that belonged to his grandfather and has a vegetable garden.

Huckleberry Finn

There are two Richard Scarrys, father and son. **Richard Scarry** senior was an American children's author and illustrator who published over 300 children's books with over 100 million sales worldwide. He was born in Boston where his father ran a department store. Richard moved with his family to Switzerland in 1968 and settled in Gstaad where he later died aged 74.

Throughout his life whenever he was asked how old he was, he always answered five. Some thought it was a joke, others politely changed the subject. But, it was true! According to his son his inner world was peopled by animals such as dogs, cats, bears, owls as well as foxes, rabbits and his very favourite pigs. These animal characters were basically people through whom he told stories and conveyed information. And he proved quite adept at giving human characteristics to a seemingly endless number of creatures. Many elements of Switzerland found their way into his illustrations be they chalets, clothing or lake steamers.

Richard Scarry junior aka Huck has continued his father's oeuvre through creating new books based on his father's characters. Huck began helping his father as teenager assisting him

Richard Scarry

colouring up on *Cars, Trucks and Things That Go.*

He wrote and illustrated numerous books on his own but when his father had trouble with his eyesight, Huck helped him out. Then when his father died in 1994, Huck decided to work full-time looking after his father's oeuvre and creating new books with his characters.

Here was also serendipity. In 2014, he discovered tracing paper sketches under his father's desk which he brought to completion as the *Best Lowly Worm Book Ever.* When he works, he always feels his father's presence strongly and often hears him laugh.

Huck was characterised by his father first as *Huckle Bear, Huckle Cat and then Lowly Worm* and became an extension of his father's personality. When not working on his father's books, Huck loves to draw watercolours. He did a series of four travel books about Italy for Mondadori. A talented watercolorist, he gives courses every summer in Greece.

"There's a photo of me as a baby being held by my father," said Huck, an affable and courtly man, "It was then that I was first called Huck because, he thought, I looked like a real Huckleberry Finn."

Huck Finn was one of Richard senior's favourite characters of the author Mark Twain. Consequently, he made his son into one of his book characters: the original Huckle was a 'lederhosen-toting bear' who later became a 'lederhosen-toting cat.' Huckle cat's best friend is a worm called Lowly who wears a Tyrolean hat.

"My parents met at a party in Greenwich Village and were married within two weeks," said Huck. "My mother, a stunning woman, Patricia Murphy, was at the time writing advertising copy in New York. She found that she also had a talent for writing for children. My father discovered he had a talent for drawing for children and they made numerous books together such as *Good Night, Little Bear* and *The Bunny Book* which was dedicated to me as a baby."

Richard senior's iconic book, *The Best Word Book Ever* was published in 1963 by Golden Books and sold over one million copies. The book is crammed with some 1,400 objects for inquisitive children to discover and learn.

"One of the reasons my father's books are successful is that he speaks directly to children and only draws what he would like to see there himself," he said. "This book was a turning point in his life as it was the first time he did a book entirely on his own without a commission. He got the idea from the Duden picture dictionary and thought he could do something similar for children."

"He was the best father ever because he spent time with me and was more like a brother than a father," he continued. "As a child I'd lie on my father's studio floor – it smelled of sharpened pencils and rubber cement and paper, drawing alongside him."

If there is a philosophy that Huck abides by it's a line by John Lennon: "Life is what happens while you're busy making other plans." He gives an example of his daughter Katja: "She had just finished teachers training college in Vienna and was sitting on a bus in Budapest with her colleagues talking about their future plans. A man in the seat in front of her turned around and asked if they were schoolteachers. He explained he had just become the director of a German-speaking elementary school in Hungary and was looking for teachers. Katja thought the offer over and accepted."

Huck met his first wife, Marlis, in New York. She was not at first very happy to encounter him. She had returned from a trip and found that the apartment she had been promised was suddenly occupied by a strange man. Huck met his second wife, Gaby while he was drawing in the Café Hawelka in Vienna. A couple entered and sat at a table he was drawing. He hesitated and then decided to draw the couple at the table. "What are you doing!," asked the young lady turning to Huck. He showed her the drawing and that was that.

Huck splits the year between homes in Vienna and Gstaad and in between, he teaches watercolouring in Greece on the island of Zakynthos. This is a highlight in his calendar as his students are relaxed yet eager and concentrated which makes teaching fun.

Huck's children are all very creative and art forms an important aspect of their lives. Fiona lives in London and has several creative talents: she has worked as a stylist for fashion magazines, film and theatre as well as in art galleries. Olympia is an artist. She co-curates Gstaad's biannual winter art event Elevation 1049 which the Anzeiger von Saanen has described as "young, sporty and cheeky." (See separate entry, Mūller Medien AG). Katja is an elementary schoolteacher in Vienna, and Julian is studying fashion design in London.

Suddenly a House Appears

"Now that my kids are grown up, I'm looking forward to spending still more time in Saanenland," he said. "I love hiking and skiing. My parents bought our chalet in 1974. We've done some renovation but the chalet remains much as it did then; a cosy little place packed with books, papers, and drawings. When we first saw it, the living room reminded us of a captain's cabin on an old sailing ship. The downstairs was and is a creative chaotic working studio.

The house has a peculiar story to it. It was built by a woodcarver and his son on a small empty plot next to where they lived. Simple as that. The lady who actually owned the land returned one day to find the new house there. When she enquired from her neighbours about it they intimated that it was a free piece of land. As she was philosophical and a generous soul, and amused by the chutzpah of these locals, she allowed the house to remain on her land with the only proviso that once it was sold, she should be reimbursed.

There are two Richard Scarrys but they both agree with having fun in their lives. They believe that if you're not having fun in your work you're doing something wrong.

Woman Engineer

Ombretta Ravessoud made her mark in a man's world twice in her life. But one should not be surprised

Ombretta Ravessoud

because she is talented, intelligent, personable and yet very feminine. The first occasion was when she was one of the first woman students at the Ecole d'Ingénieurs Geneva. The second time was when she worked for the electrical engineering giant, Brown Boveri Baden (now ABB) as sales manager for electric traction. Today, she has completed the circle and runs an art gallery, is editor-in-chief of an art magazine, Artpassions, as well as a co-founder of a music festival, Sommets Musicaux de Gstaad.

"I was born in Brescia where my father was an industrialist and made objects out of tin," she said. "We came to Geneva when I was seven. My world was the artists like Michelangelo, Brancusi, Schiele and Modigliani. But I had no gift for drawing or painting. I was good at mathematics and physics. So after my baccalaureate, I studied engineering at the Engineering school Geneva and gained a diploma in electrotechnics. My first job was at Brown Boveri where I worked with the Montreux Oberland Bern (MOB) railway and first came to Gstaad. I also attended courses at EPFL." She paused and then smiled as her eyes brightened and added: "I was proud of being the only woman to work among the men who were kind enough to help me succeed."

Her breakthrough came in 1992 when she founded Sport Art management company, SAM SA. She organised sports events such as the triathlon in Geneva which is for professional athletes who want to compete in the Olympics or other championships and the multi-discipline competition in Crans Montana. Today, it has morphed into 'Le Terrific' for young and old athletes with seven disciplines such as mountain biking, ski mountaineering, vertical climbing, swimming, road cycling and running.

"In 1999, I co-founded with Thierry Scherz, the Sommets Musicaux de Gstaad," she said. "It was a musical highlight of the winter season for classical lovers and among the sponsors was Bank Edmond de Rothschild. I enjoyed many 'Wow' performances such as the violinist Renaud Capuçon, our artistic director and the pianists Martha Argerich, David Fray and Andras Schiff. I'm proud that it has continued for some 19 years."

Her next big venture was the foundation of Artpassions with Jean-Pierre Möri which was established in 2005. It's a published quarterly and devoted to art and culture. The goal is to provide art news in all its forms from painting, sculpture, design, photography and architecture as well as music and cinema.

"When I was a girl my parents gave me a subscription to an Italian art magazine, *I Maestri del Colore* "she said, "and I always wanted to do something in that field. One of my memorable occasions was the interview with Ernst Beyeler in his office in central Basel. He was a kind, charismatic figure and what impressed me was his height as he almost reached the low ceiling of the room."

John of God

Dominique Rossignol-Franck is one of those people who search for truth in life and find answers. She is a historian and music lover and her path was always strewn with books and music. She is Secretary-General of the Committee of the Friends at the Sommets Musicaux, Gstaad, organises films of the operas from the Metropolitan New York at the cinema Eden in Chateau d'Oex and is a member of the scientific council of the double museum in Paris dedicated to

Dominique Rossignol-Franck

General Leclerc who liberated the city and Jean Moulin, the Resistance leader.

"My father was a publisher who had two imprints, Denoël and Planet," she said, "which stimulated my wide interest in books, specially autobiographies and personal quests such as Herman Melville's novel, Moby Dick, among others. I was bored at school because my world of books and music stretched far beyond the horizon of the classroom's program. My music education began by listening to the package of classical records we received every year. I was introduced to Pergolesi's Stabat Mater, all Mozart's operas, Russia composers particularly Prokofiev's piano concertos and I was stunned by Wagner's Valkyrie at the age of 15. I also became a fan of Maria Callas as a child when I heard her sing in the theatre on the side of the Parthenon in Athens. It was a revelation of her fascinating voice."

She was educated at Dupanloup, a former religious school in Paris and later gained a PhD in history at Paris university. Her thesis was on disruptive periods in France such as the revolution of 1848 and Vichy in World War II. She is the author of several books including *Vichy et les Francs-maçons: La liquidation des sociétés secrètes, 1940-1944* (1981), *Histoire de la propagande en France de 1940 à 1944, l'utopie Pétain* (1991) and *Les manifestations visibles de l'au-delà* (2018).

"What I found surprising as a historian was the treatment of the Vichy period," she said. "It was glossed over and Petain was hailed as a saviour. It provoked me to write on the subjects like Vichy's propaganda machine and the liquidation of secret societies. Finally the record was set straight by Jacques Chirac the French president who denounced the role played by French citizens and the collaborative Vichy government who deported some 76,000 Jews."

"After graduating from university, I travelled to India with the mission of finding the first text of humanity, of the creation of God," she continued. "It was important to know the works of the great sages of India. When I returned, I met Eric Franck. It was a coup de foudre. We opened a gallery together and started a family. After ten years of existence the gallery closed during the Gulf war crisis in 1991 and I became ill with an intestine complaint. I had several operations but could not be cured in spite of being treated in Swiss hospitals as well as the Mayo clinic in the US."

In desperation, she searched for alternative possibilities all around the world. She consulted shamans from Siberia and Canada as she felt she was too young to die. Then someone suggested the healer, John of God (Joao de Deus) in Abadiania, Brazil who initiated Casa de Dom Inacio de Loyola in 1979 as a spiritual healing centre. He works as a full trance medium and has left his body to the good spirits as a tool to enable healing. The first spirit being (or 'entity') that was incorporated into Joao de Deus's body was King Solomon. "I have never healed anyone," he said. "It's God who heals." The Casa is not far from the capital Brasilia. It's located on a plateau at 1,052m above sea level and was built on a crystal soil that supports and enhances the healing energy of the spirits.

"The Casa is a place of love and I was there for three weeks," she said. "The treatment is free and I spent most of the time in the meditation rooms. Some times you pass in front of John of God and he often tells you to work on yourself. Sometimes, he asks for volunteers to do a visible operation which involves sticking a knife into an arm. The day after there is no scar or sign of a wound as it has all disappeared."

On her return, some time later all the symptoms had vanished. It was the beginning of synchronicity in herself. Her life revolves more than ever around music which she discovers in the sound of the sea crashing on the sand or the wind moving the branches. If there is anything that she subscribes to it's Shakespeare's quote from Twelfth Night: "If music be the food of love, play on, give me excess of it.."

Her last book, Les manifestations visibles de l'au-delà (The Visible Manifestations from the beyond), is an extraordinary journey taken after her miraculous healing. It is a perfect circle as it answers the questions on god and the universe she sought as a young woman on her visits to India, Nepal and spiritual lands.

Through her documented scientific analysis, she enables readers to discover phenomena which are both invisible to the naked eye and yet visible in photos. For her, these are signs of the world of spirits that surround us. In a way, it also explains ancient secrets pertaining to Greek myths. For example, Demeter and Persephone which was celebrated as the Eleusinian Mysteries in which Persephone is abducted from her mother, Demeter, by the king of the underworld, Hades and then returned once a year. What if the ancient Greeks had similar mediums such Joao de Deus who were in contact with spirits and could heal people.

Positive Attitude

Walter Egger is the president of Gstaad airport and the owner of Egger Engineering. In his engineering capacity, he is a one-stop shop with his team of seven which includes civil engineers, draftsmen and designers. His diverse projects cover infrastructure of roads, channelisation of rivers, constructing foundations according to earthquake regulations, building tunnels, airfields and individual chalets.

"I grew up in Sargans in the canton of St.Gallen and after I gained my engineering diploma, I was offered several jobs in different parts of Switzerland," he said. "But my girlfriend Barbara (now my wife), and I were taken by Saanenland and we decided to stay for three years. But we liked the people and the place so much that we've been here for over 40 years. As Saanenland is the countryside, I had to be flexible with small projects and started working with architects and entrepreneurs, In 1980, I established my own practice."

Walter was involved in the four year construction of the Grand Hotel Alpina in which the excavation was filled with 4,000 tons of reinforcing steel and 40,000 cubic metres of concrete. Another exciting project was the Glacier 3000 where the job

Walter Egger

was to transport water from a lake to snowmaking equipment. It required heli-transport of machinery, pipes and diggers as well as deep sea divers to lay the pipes under the lake. It is one of the several projects where the latest technology is used.

"One of the community projects, I'm proud to be part of is the CHF 30 million new airport," said Walter who is the president of the airport co-operative Gstaad-Saanenland (FGGS). "The airport was established during the Second World War and was used by the military until1980s when it was handed over for civilian use. The new airport includes five hangers, among them are three for the private aircraft, one for utilities like the fire brigade and snow removal equipment and another for Air Glacier the helicopter company. It will improve greatly the facilities offered in winter to private aircraft arrivals and departures."

The key element is the new terminal which consists of a wooden building and the cost of renewing the infrastructure and the building was CHF 30 million. According to Marcel Bach, a committee member, one half was raised by private funding and the remainder through the Saanenland municipality, FOCA(Federal Office of Civil Aviation) and Bern Canton. (See entry, Marcel Bach.)

"I've always been impressed by is the positive attitude of the people in Saanenland," said Walter. "I was the president of the Tourism Board for 10 years and each group whether they were farmers, industry or members of the tourism board all pulled together and shared consensus about issues. But there was also another aspect which I should mention. They never standstill because they are a progressive people and move on to the next project which is a multifunctional centre for conferences and concerts."

Champion Skier

From outward appearance, **Bethli Küng-Marmet** is a typical woman from Saanenland or as she refers to herself, a Saanen Geiss (goat) which is the symbol for the village. She became a teacher, married, had children and

Bethli Küng-Marmet

served in the local community. But when you talk to her, you find she had an interesting life. She was born in the oldest house in the village which dates back to 1556 and survived the fire in the 16th century. When she left school, she was told by her teacher that she would never learn English. But her determination, a feature of her character, later won through.

"Once I'd qualified as a teacher, I was offered an au pair job by a family in Stamford, Connecticut who paid a return ticket," she said. "I had 15 weeks summer holiday so I took the opportunity. When I told my father who was a dairy farmer, he was beside himself and said I was crazy because

America was so far away that I'd never come back. I should have gone to England instead to learn English. But it worked out well and I was amazed by everything and brought back a pair of blue jeans. My only regret was when I arrived in New

York, I couldn't ring my parents as they already had gone up to the alps with the cows where there was no electricity and only basic accommodation. So I sent them a postcard instead."

Police Chief

Bethli which is a diminutive of Elisabeth was very sporty and while still at school made the Swiss national team. She came first in the special Slalom and combination and although, selected to represent Switzerland at Grenoble in 1968, she missed the Winter Olympics due to a broken thigh. She married Chlaus Küng, the police chief of Gstaad and had two children.

In winter, she was in demand as a ski teacher, in particular with the Goulandris family whom she has been with for the past 30 years. She taught their children, cousins, extended family as well as some of the illustrious guests such as the Kings Constantine of Greece and Juan Carlos of Spain.

"It was only when my three children (Vera, Rolf and Klaus), were old enough that I got involved in politics," she said. "In 1989, I was elected to the municipal council, the only woman among 12 men. Nine years later, I became a member of the grand council for the canton Bern representing Saanenland and Ober Simmental. One of the issues that I championed was the building of a new road between Zweisimmen and Gstaad. It was a shame as there was only a cow path that led to the biggest touristic centre in Bern canton. In 2000, I became the first woman to be elected president in the history of Saanen commune."

She also motivated young women to have a profession and careers. One girl, Alexandra, whom she took under her wing was studying to be a salesgirl. Her parents were divorced and she offered her a room in her home. After two years she wanted to give up but Bethli encouraged her to complete her course.

A Club is Like a Family

The commodore of the Gstaad Yacht Club (GYC) is a genial Italian, **Manrico Iachia** who was born in Bologna. He studied business and politics at Milan university and his military service was spent in a tank. He joined Generali Insurance and his career took him to five continents. He learnt to sail in Greece with friends on 18m sailing boats.

"I heard about the GYC at a dinner party here in Gstaad," he said. "At the time, I was living in Portugal close to the sea and I enjoying boating. As a classic car and Riva nut, I joined after having taken part in the first Rally

Manrico Iachia

and Yachting event. This event will celebrate its 10th anniversary this summer in 2019. The destination is the best kept secret – water is involved, as all participants, after a scenic drive, perform model boat sailing on a lake or sea."

If there is anything he is proud of, its the new reciprocities he organised with 25 yacht clubs worldwide. His opening gambit was simple. "Do you want to be a member of a unique global yacht club away from the water, instead of another local club by the water." The clubs offer GYC members a global network of friends and give Gstaad the opportunity to welcome an interesting flow of international guests.

"During the 25 years with Generali, the quickest way to connect with the locals was to join a club," he said with a smile. "It's like becoming a member of a family. That's what we have at the GYC and being an Italian it's something I appreciate. Another thing I enjoy, is pasta."

Cabanas by the Cold Sea

But there is another side to Manrico's life. He is a pioneer in developing the Portuguese beach town, Comporta, an hour south of Lisbon and in three decades became an architectural showcase. Manrico's wife, Vera, a member of the Espírito Santo banking dynasty and interior designer had created cabanas, freestanding buildings with woven-reed facades and palm-covered gable-sided roofs. Later it became known as the Simplicity-

Comporta style and attracted the international crowd like Anselm Kiefer, Princess Caroline and Albert of Monaco, Christian Louboutin and Philippe Starck to an area of natural beauty and quiet isolation.

"When we first came here some 30 years ago," said Manrico, "swarms of mosquitoes rose from the rice fields like black clouds at dusk. White-sand dunes stretched for miles and the ocean was turquoise. Driving through the area past farmer's fields there were whitewashed villages and the occasional glimpse of the water."

Vera Iachia, was born in Lisbon and studied at Parsons School of Design in New York. She began her career working for Andy Warhol, who presented her to the world of Pop Art. She went on to work with the top French interior designer, Jacques Grange, in Paris, whom she had introduced to Comporta and who became another major pillar of the area, before she returned to Lisbon and established her own interior design consultancy. Sadly, she died in 2017.

Christine Lang Camerana

Christine Lang Camerana is a prominent resident of Gstaad and a keen skier. She first set eyes on the resort when she came on holidays as her parents always rented chalets and consequently learnt to ski there. Later, she came as a boarder to Montesano school for girls in Gstaad. She has a

Christine Lang Camerana

great sense of belonging as she also met her husband Count Vittorio Camerana when he went to visit his brother Marco who was a student at Le Rosey. Today, she is the doyenne of social events at the Gstaad Yacht Club.

"Some of my fondest memories as a girl was arriving at Gstaad station and being picked up by a sleigh drawn by horses," said Christine an elegant tall woman, "and gliding along the snow covered roads up to the chalet. By then Le Rosey had been founded as a boarding school for boys. Our treat was dancing on Saturday nights when we were allowed to mix with the boys. Not many people know that the resort was first discovered by the Belgians and that people like Baron Leon Lambert, the banker, would leave Brussels by Wagonlit on a Friday night and spend Saturday skiing in Gstaad before returning on Sunday."

After her marriage, Christine and her husband went to live in Turin where they had two sons. She has been back in Gstaad for the past two decades and became actively in involved with the Gstaad Yacht Club. She also gained a reputation as a good skier and goes most off- piste on ski touring.

"One of the things I'm proud of achieving at the Club is introducing new members," she said. "I've invited people from different countries to come to events and they've enjoyed the ambiance and the facilities so much that they've joined. Currently, we're running about 400 members. Of course, I have all sorts of events and one which was most interesting was the reading of love letters by a friend, Anne-Marie Springer, who has one of the largest collections - some 2,000, including Frédéric Chopin, Winston Churchill, James Joyce, Elvis Presley, Napoleon and Frida Kahlo."

When Christine reached the venerable age of 80, she decided to stop skiing. Instead she hikes and has returned to a pastime for exercise she knew well as a schoolgirl: dancing. In her case it's not to popular songs with a partner but to jazz music in which she improvises the movements.

Karolos and Athina Fix

Some 25% of the population of Saanenland are foreigners who have chalets and visit periodically. Some like Karolos and Athina Fix have chosen to live here permanently. Their two children first went to school at JKF and Le Rosey and then they decided to settle too. Karolos who used to run Fix Asset Management which manages assets of €12 million in 300 funds, first skied in Gstaad as a teenager. Later, he studied chemistry at Lausanne university. He owns an Embraer E190-E2 jet and Gstaad airport is convenient for his trips.

"I'm a psychologist and see thing objectively and I'm not judgemental," said Athina aka Ninetta. I was trained in the US and worked at a university. "My first impressions of Gstaad were positive. I believe you can judge a country by the way they treat their animals. I was sitting in Charly's when we first arrived and my dog was next to me on the floor. The waitress came up and said 'put the dog near you on the sofa.' I was impressed because in time I came to realise that the Swiss were nice people and respect your privacy, and you can live a high quality life in the country.'"

Ninetta and her husband came from Greece in 1982 when the Socialist government nationalised the Fix family's brewery. They originally came from Bavaria but they followed King Otto, the first King of the Greeks, to Greece.

Karl Johann Georg Fix founded the famous brewery in 1864.

"My favorite time is the low season in March and September when have the mountains to ourselves," she said. "Everyone is gone and we locals are happy to see each other. Contacts are more personal and intense when the village is not crowded with tourists. I love the tranquility of the mountains too. The valley is shaped like a huge hug and I feel snug in its embrace."

When they first arrived in Gstaad some 40 years ago, there were wonderful parties and everyone including the celebrities had fun. Nowadays, people are more discrete and tend to have small intimate functions. Even at the Palace, things have calmed down except for the lobby which is still the place to be seen until the small hours. Gstaad is also on the radar for international social caravan that flies in at the high season and Le Rosey's long weekend that attracts some 800-1,000 alumni. The Gstaad Yacht Club is an important element in the social life as it organises cultural events throughout the year.

"I've found the locals to be wise," Ninetta said. "A farmer who taught me to ski doesn't want his children to become doctors or lawyers but rather plumbers or electricians. It seems cool as careers in the future an change radically, the basic needs will be in greater demand."

Laurence Graff

Laurence Graff started in London's jewellery quarter and today he is a billionaire businessman who has handled more important diamonds than any other person on earth. He produces the finest diamonds and high jewellery showcased in a retail empire of jewellery boutiques worldwide.

Graff was born in the East End of London to parents of Russian-Romanian descent. While his father was away during the war, his mother ran a sweet shop and it was here that he was introduced to commerce.

"I left school and became a jeweller's apprentice," he said. "At first I was told I would never make it, but that just made me more determined. I worked hard and decided to go into business myself at the age of 17. I get a thrill every morning when I open a package of rough diamonds, polished diamonds or coloured precious stones and marvel at the light that emanates, the life inside each one and their potential."

Laurence has built a business with strong family values. His son Francois is the CEO of the company while his brother Raymond, has managed the Graff workshop and his nephew Elliott directs procurement, merchandising and production.

"As my business grew, I acquired larger and rarer stones," he said, "and our jewellery creations increased in value. I began to make a name for myself and

Laurence Graff

business leader in the industry, Harry Oppenheimer, gave me some advice. He said that to get ahead, I should align myself with all stages of the process, from sourcing of the rough to the making of the jewellery. So we acquired a polishing business and never looked back."

Graff has successfully polished the majority of the world's most important rough diamonds discovered this century, including the largest gem quality diamond found in over 100 years: the Lesedi La Rona at 1,109cts. Many of these have in turn, yielded famous polished diamonds such as the 118.78ct Graff Venus, the 118.08ct Delaire Sunrise and the 102.79ct Graff Constellation, each global sensations, breaking records for their size and quality.

"I love being surrounded by beautiful things whether it be a precious gem or an art masterpiece," he said. "I am passionate about art and have built a collection that began in the 70's with a small Renoir that I used to keep in a safe with my diamonds."

Graff was the first jeweller to win the Queen's award for industry in 1973. He was awarded the OBE in 2013. He has never forgotten his humble upbringing where he learnt honesty and correctness and if there is a word to describe his philosophy, it's respect - the respect for others.

Chapter 2. Bakers

Great homemade bread and mouthwatering patisserie.

"R" Chocolate Boutique

Viktoriastrasse 3
Tel 033 748 3580
infor@chocolateboutique.ch

Stefan Romang is the grandmaster of pastry and chocolates in Gstaad, a judge in international competitions that encourage young talent and a former owner of Charly's tearoom who brought it to new level of elegance through his modernisation. Together with his wife Heidi, they run the small, high-end handmade chocolate and pastry boutique. The pastries in the shop are out of this world. They are light and exquisite and his signature is the mille-feuille. The chocolates are mouth-watering and made only out of premium cocoa beans, the grand cru, from the best growing regions. His signature is the truffle and the griottes with cherry brandy. The other delicacy is the home smoked salmon with no additives or artificial flavours. It's marinated for two days in a herb-vegetable mixture and was awarded the coveted Scottish label "Rouge."

"I don't talk dark chocolate here," said Stefan, a jovial man who wears a panama hat from Ecuador. "I talk homemade grand cru from Madagascar, Bolivia and Ecuador. We have an exclusivity to buy the small production, some 10-12 tons, of the Bolivian Wild coco bean. And we don't talk pastry, we talk crispy puff pastry. It's airy crème with a subtle vanilla flavour and we put the cuts together differently. Consequently, there's less contact of the cream with the puff pastry which remains crispy. We have also replaced the icing with powdered sugar to make our cream slices lighter, wholesome and finer."

Stefan was born in Gstaad where his father was a carpenter who specialised in mouldings and trims. He went to the local school and had an apprenticeship as a confectioner. He worked for the best chocolatier Wuthrich in Lausanne and also learnt French. After his military service, he started at the Palace,

Heidi and Stefan Romang

Gstaad where became chief patisseur. (1986-1994). As it was seasonal - open only for six months, he travelled the world for the rest of the time.

"It was crazy period for me as I had my first trip on a plane and saw a big city like Buenos Aires," he said. "But I worked all the time and picked up local recipes that used tropical fruits like mangoes which we didn't have here. Once I spent a summer in a Stockholm restaurant and others in Paris, Thailand and Chile where I learnt about smoking salmon. Then I met Heidi, the highlight of my life, in the Landhaus, Saanen. She knew everyone as she worked at the Berg restaurant Eggli."

Cakes are made to order and can include a big crayfish or even a space cake with a rocket weighing 15kgs and made out of chocolate mousse. But the range of products varies from sandwiches, mini-pastries, modern cakes to chocolate specialities.

"I can't emphasise enough that I live my profession to the full," he said. "I use the best ingredients and my long experience and expertise is used to make our creations unique delights that our clients love so much."

Charly's Gstaad AG

Promenade 76
Tel. 033 744 1544
info@charlys-gstaad.ch
www.charlys-gstaad.ch

Charly's which is an institution in Gstaad, is one of the hot spots during the high season, the other being the Lobby at the Palace at midnight. (See separate entry, Stephan Romang). Charly's is the place to drink coffee or quaff wine on the terrace which abuts the Promenade or tuck into a crémeschnitte while seated in the prime areas at the bar or near the windows overlooking the ice rink. Other guests like Tara Bernerd, the designer known for elegantly masculine interiors, begins her Saturday mornings reading newspapers at Charly's. Above all, it's the locale to people-watch or to be seen.

The coffee shop's interior is contemporary alpine decor with a luxury ambiance. There is a cornucopia of homemade patisserie and confectionery delights. It includes almond topping, yogurt creations, vermicelles, millefeuilles, berries, carac, fruit cake, brownies, apple strudel and of course, bread, croissant and lemon tea. But there's also the selection of healthy food like salads and soups as well as different milks including almond, soja and lactose-free.

"Our club sandwich and crêpes (salty and sweet) are very popular," said Christa Hauswirth, the manager. "We serve Illy coffee, espresso and cappuccino as well as latte macchiato. The chocolate mousse cake and the flannet, a thin tart with pears are delicious. But a 'must' is the homemade hot chocolate with whipped cream. It's just the thing after a day of skiing or hiking."

Chnusper-Becke

Dorfstrasse 32
3778 Schönried
Tel. 0337441484
info@chnusper-becke.ch

Dubidorfweg 1
3780 Gstaad
Tel. 033 744 1324
info@chnusper-becke.ch

The two bakeries are a boon to the people both visitors and locals because they are one-stop shop and open seven days a week in the high season. The selection of breads is amazing - some 30 different varieties and they are organic and baked on the premises. Coffee and takeaway sandwiches are also popular.

"Schönried is a real village because it has a butcher, a baker and a shop selling milk products," said Andrea Wehren who is the 5th generation owner. "It encourages people to socialise while they do their shopping."

There are also two unusual chocolates to try or use as gifts. The kisses or Saanenland Müntscheni have a filling of meringue and hazel nuts while

Andrea Wehren

the Saanensenf praline which has a cherry filling, comes in a lovely box decorated with Swiss paper cutouts of landscapes or Sherenschnitte that make ideal souvenirs. Highlights of patisserie includes pineapple pastry filled with pineapple cream and a Swiss favourite of ovomaltine filling. The staff's motto is friendliness and expertise with excellent service. Consequently, they try to meet the most demanding customers's wishes.

"We take great care over our bread making," said Andrea."We ensure that no chemicals are used, make our own yeast and for our ruch bread which is popular with the locals, we use a larger part of the grain husk. Another technique is to allow the dough to

Saanensenf praline.

rest twice during the process either for an hour or a day. This increases the aroma."

The selection of food is based on the use of as many local products as possible. The meat, cheese, milk and yogurt are all from Saanenland. They have added a selection of homemade pizzas and pies as well as tinned food such as corned beef which is a staple for farmers when they are in the Alps in summer. Andrea's mother, Vreni Wehren is responsible for all non-bakery products and her favourite food is Züri Geschnetzeltes mit Rösti.

"There never was any doubt in my mind to follow in the footsteps of my father, Ernst," she said. "My parents were so happy working together seven days a week. I was fortunate also because my father was a bakery teacher and had a talent for education. So when I did my apprenticeship at our bakery, I learnt by heart a baker's logic."

As a girl, the first thing Andrea learnt was to twist the dough for the milk bread. She was keen on sales and with the money she earned, saved up to buy a moped for fun. Andrea has three siblings one of whom, Beat, also became baker in Weggis on lake Lucerne.

The bakeries which are owned by Andrea were started by her great great grandfather, Gottlieb and his wife Emilie Dubi who came from St Stephan, Bern canton and opened a bakery in Gstaad.

Cafe and Délice Chocolateur

Dorfstrasse 4
Saanen
Tel. 033744 4001
info@delicecafe.ch
www.delicecafe.ch

Délice cafe is a wow because the interior design is cool contemporary. It's open plan with three different spaces - conventional tables and chairs, a boardroom table for business discussions and a family area with settees and a play section. Outside there is a choice of two terraces - one with a hanging bench! Chocolates, wedding and birthday cakes are the stars at Délice. There are other things in-between. The cafe has a great selection of coffees, teas, Délice drinking chocolate, bagels with all sorts of fillings and they also serve simple and nourishing dishes such as salads, soups and pasta. It is also a popular breakfast place where deluxe and simple breakfasts are offered.

"Délice is the realisation of a dream of which Reto and I had," aid Heidi Sigrist-Wehren, "to create a place for people to come together, have conversations, meetings and a lot of pleasure. We want their visit to be a delight right from our friendly service to our homemade products."

When they met the architect, Hanspeter Reichenbach, it all came together. Heidi is a talented pastry chef who won several competitions

Délice.

as a junior and then in 2003 became a world champion in the Worldskills event. Reto has a master certificate in pastry-confectionery and is a passionate chocolate specialist. He worked at Schuh, the famous chocolateria in Interlaken.

"My father, Ruedi Wehren, is a dairy farmer and in summer I would accompany my parents to the alps where they made cheese,"she said."I enjoyed serving visitors who came to see us with plates of cheese or milk. My mother was a good cook and inspired me with her apfelstrudel with vanilla cream." (See separate entry, Wehren).

Heidi grew up in Gstaad and met her husband Reto during their apprenticeship at Charly's. (See separate entry, Charly's) Her metier is unique cakes for exclusive parties and society weddings. Clients bring her ideas which she implements. Requests for children's birthdays include ducks or an intricate designs of tractors and lorries on top of the cake or just a flat, green long fish.

"After I won the awards, I was happy but skeptical of my new celebrity,"she said."My response was so what! I had many questions about the meaning of life. I needed something more relevant in my life and I found it in religion. I know we are not alone and the Lord thinks of a good future for me and my family and gives us hope."

Heidi and Reto have two daughters.

Chapter 3. Shopping

Big brands to die for and great local discoveries.

Buure Metzg AG

Alte Lauenenstrasse 10
Tel. 033744 1144
gstaad@buuremetz.ch
www.buuremetz.ch

When customers step in here they are in another world of butchers. Some say it's a gourmet's paradise. Robert Bratschi, the master butcher, offers a wide assortment of things you never expect to find: fish, cheese, ice cream, diary products, fruit, vegetables, wine and pan-ready or a traiteur assortment. Then there's the pièce de résistance, the meat. The selection varies from bone-aged meat (côte de bœuf, T-bone, entrecôte), homemade (raw ham, coppa, mostbröckli, bacon, sausage pies and terrines), charcuterie (cold cuts, Buureschinken, dry sausage, salami) and pre-cooked dishes which can be heated at home as well as cold prepared plates (pâtés/terrines, antipasti, salads and apèro finger food).

"Our butcher shop is unique," said Robert Bratschi, "it's a one-stop shop with everything visitors and chalet owners can want. Our concept been a great success. During Christmas and New Year we're also open on Sundays. My team includes my wife, Marlise, who supervises all the non-meat products and runs the administration and my daughter Elvira."

Robert Bratschi was born in Gstaad and followed in the footsteps of his father who was a freelance butcher and slaughtered animals on farms. He served an apprenticeship with Ruedi Matti who is the oldest inhabitant of Gstaad at 98 and traded from the same address. In 1996, Robert and his wife Marlise together with Martin Hauswirth and his wife Nicole took over the butcher shop of Ruedi Matti on Alte Lauenenstrasse in Gstaad. Two other butcher shops were acquired in Schönried which is run by Martin and Nicole and in Rougemont. Robert has been a butcher for almost 40 years and is always smiling.

"With our branches in Schönried and Rougemont we're the only butchers in Saanenland and use only local meat," he

Buure Metzg.

said, "because we know where it comes from and even in some cases the name of the cow. The exceptions are at peak times when entrecôte and fillet have to be bought from Emmental. Our hits are bone matured meat, dried raw ham, coppa, dried meat, bacon and mostbröckli. They are prepared in a special drying room in Lauenen by Rolf von Siebenthal until they have reached an ideal consistency and taste. They have also won several gold medals by the Swiss Meat Federation."

Other innovations include deliveries to chalets of specially stuffed turkeys prior to Christmas and an automatic meat dispenser outside the butcher shop. The highest demand at the dispenser happens between 1am to 3am when people leave the night clubs.

"You don't become a butcher unless you have a passion because you work hard, sometimes for 11 hours," he said. "We're up at 5am and open at 6am. I'm proud and grateful that all the hotels and restaurants are good customers which is a recognition of their appreciation of high quality. My favourites are osso bucco and slow cooked meat dishes. For relaxation, I like golf and fishing and we like to go to the German seaside resort of Rugen for holidays."

Molkerei Gstaad

Lauenenstrasse 24
3780 Gstaad
Tel. 033 744 11 15
info@molkerei-gstaad.ch
www.molkerei-gstaad.ch

René Ryser, the king of cheese.

The quickest way to step into the ancient tradition of dairy farming in the Alps is to taste the range of cheeses, yogurts and milk at the Molkerei Gstaad. Most of the milk comes from Simmental cows which produce the famous meat in Switzerland and graze in the Saanenland meadows at 1,000m where flowers, grasses and herbs proliferate. This rich pasturage gives the Alpkäse a distinctive flavour, a real taste of Swiss mountains. The cheese is made with raw milk and is lactose-free.

"I recommend three cheeses as a start," said René Ryser, a master cheesemaker of almost 40 years and nicknamed the King of Cheese. "Alpkäse, Mutschli - a raclette type and Rhamli - a small cheese like a tomme. For those who like to enjoy a cheese with wine, I would suggest a Hobel cheese drunk with a white Johannisberg. They make a perfect marriage."

Alpkäse is a firm, strong cheese which has an intense earth flavour and is always produced by ancient methods in a giant copper kettle. When aged for several years, the cheese is known as hobelkäse. In the Berner Oberland, it's always served in thinly, shaved slices.

Other favourites of the locals include goats cheese, the local butter which is apparently rich in omega 3 fatty acids, whey or zigger which is full of protein and is usually eaten with jam because of its tasteless flavour. Fondue and raclette are the main dishes of the region and equipment for making fondue can be found in the souvenir corner of the molkerei. There are also wooden cows and baskets with fabric covers to keep potatoes warm for raclette.

The Molkerei is the showcase for dairy products of the Gstaad Co-operative which represents 74 farmers from the district and stocks 3,000 wheels of Hobelkäse which are kept at an optimum temperature in an underground storage facility. Visits to the storage facility, an exceptional experience, is by appointment and can be accompanied by a cheese tasting. Jürg Romang whose family has kept herds of Simmental is the president of the co-operative.

Patricia Low Contemporary

Parkstrasse
Tel. 033 7448804
patricia@patricialow.com
www.patricialow.com

When it comes to contemporary art, Patricia Low is the place to go. Since she started in 2005, her focus has

An ad for Jeff Koons' new edition sculptures showing at Patricia's gallery in Gstaad.

been to introduce the most prominent international artists with an emphasis on the legacies of Neue Wilde, Contemporary German Painting, Young British Art, Contemporary Photography, Post-Feminism, and Pop and putting together historic exhibitions featuring works from the secondary market. She is an art powerhouse who runs a top gallery in Gstaad.

"Key artists who have exhibited in the gallery," said Patricia, "include Wim Delvoye, Sylvie Fleury, Damien Hirst, Axel Hütte, Bjarne Melgaard, Jonathan Meese, Marc Quinn, Anselm Reyle, Chiharu Shiota, Gavin Turk, Joana Vasconcelos and Thomas Zipp. The newly emerging artists in the contemporary scene are also covered such as Jean-Baptiste Bernadet, Sebastian Hammwöhner and Gabriel Vormstein."

Although, she has a reputation as a local IT-girl, her art credentials are sound. She was born and grew up in Gstaad and after she graduated with a baccalaureate, she gained a BA in art history, journalism and economics at New York University (1994-1997). The degree was followed by a MA in art history at Brown University (1997-2000).

"I enjoy a meaningful conversation with clients," she said. "In the case of major collectors, when I know their taste I enjoy finding a special artwork for them. I once found a rare Gerhard Richter and it gave me immense satisfaction. I appreciate the intellectual pursuit because it's challenging. With newcomers to art, I dissuade them to buy on an impulse. I advise them to look at a lot of art before buying. Sometimes, it may take a year."

Hählen AG Bed & Baby

Gsteigstrasse 3
Tel. 0337441327
info@haehlen-gstaad.ch
www.haehlen-gstaad.ch

Ruedi Hählen is Mr Bed and his shop is his baby. Hählen is the leading brand for beds and baby equipment in Gstaad. If you want to be pampered at night, sleep on a custom-made mattress and not feel any aches or pains, this is the place for you. Mothers and fathers if they need to soothe their nerves about caring about baby, come here.

Ruedi Hählen is a man with a happy demeanour and is bound to smile often in conversation. He is the third generation to run the shop which was established by his grandfather, Arnold, in 1941 to sell curtains, blinds, beds and carpets. In 2002, when he took over from his parents, Ruth and Peter, he changed the shop radically. The focus is now only on beds and babies. With the beds come the mattresses, head boards and the Hählen goose down duvets. With baby you have all their paraphernalia from night gowns, toys to strollers, highchairs and car seats. But Ruedi goes the extra mile and offers visitors a rental service of baby

Grubenberghut, an alpine refuge for some 27 people.

Ruedi Hählen

equipment. So travelling won't be such a cumbersome activity.

"There are two things I'm proud of and one of them is the shop," he said with a smile. "It now totally reflects me. The ambiance is light and airy, like being outside in nature. In the renovations, I put in picture windows not only to display products but also to make it easy for people to look inside."

"The other thing I'm proud of is the Grubenberghut," he continued. "You could say I've been born with my hiking boots on. One day, my parents received a call from the Eggli cable station to inform them that their 6 year old son arrived unaccompanied at the top of the mountain (1,557 m.) I was only wearing slippers. But I've always been like that, just walking put of the house on my own on a hike somewhere. It was very natural for me. Another thing I liked to do as a boy was to sit at the window of our house and watch the weather. Asking my mother are the clouds coming in or going out? Even today I'm on the weather watch and still excited to see thunderstorms."

Ruedi was born in Gstaad above the shop where his parents live. (They are part of the team as they help from time to time with decorating or deliveries.) He wasn't much of scholar and his first job was a postman. (1982-1987). After five years he tired of the work and as he liked skiing got a job in a ski shop. It was ideal life and then he met a girl from Indiana and for two years would spend the summers there and winters back in Switzerland. The relationship ended and when he returned to Gstaad, he thought seriously about working in his parents' shop. However, he needed a background in commerce and did an apprenticeship with the Saanen bank. In 1997, he passed the banking examinations and joined the family shop. Later, he married Christine in 2001 whom he met at an old friends wedding in Frankfurt. She has masters degree in dementia care and is a team leader at an old age home in Lenk.

"My second life for the past 20 years has been the Grubenberghut which is an alpine refuge for some 27 people," he said. "It took me several years to create two major hiking trails in all directions. In total, there are now five hiking trails. The hut is like the body of a spider with five legs and there's a map on the website of the Gstaad tourism. My other career is as a guide for hiking, trekking and snowshoeing."

Ruedi knows the Saanenland and the Berner Oberland like the back of his hand. If you want an awe-inspiring experience and see magical waterfalls from Siebenbrunne (seven springs) or to be at the top of the Lenk valley with a panoramic view of the Saanenland, contact the guide par excellence. The uniqueness of Ruedi is that he always surprises his clients. Sometimes, he will open his backpack and will take out a cheese fondue or bottle of champagne as a treat.

Schuhhaus Romang

Promenade 53
Tel. 033 744 1523
welcome@schuhhaus-romang.ch
www.romang.ch
www.schuhhaus-romang.ch

Christoph Romang is the shoe king in Gstaad. At the last count before the winter season, he had 17,000 pairs in stock! The range is diverse from slippers, boots, sneakers, shoes and socks for the whole family but full of surprises. There is the ultimate in boots - seal skin at CHF 1,600 and 'must have' lambskin slippers at CHF 60.

Kandahar have produced a great boot

Christoph Romang

from sealskin which is to die for. The skins are sustainable as the Inuit in Greenland hunt to eat and use every part of the animal, even the intestines which are given to the huskies.

"I'm the third generation to own the business which was founded in 1913," said Christoph Romang. "We still have my grandfather's working table and shoe last. It's used to add crampons to shoes to prevent slipping on ice and when not needed it's bent forwards. I'm proud that on the 100th anniversary that I was able to celebrate with a new building which I own outright. I had the privilege of taking over the business in 1999 and my father Ernst and mother Esther are still on the board. It's pity that there are less and less local shops on the Promenade." (See entry, Tschanz architektur).

After school, he learnt languages - English in Cambridge, UK and French in Lausanne. Then he gained a commercial diploma and went on a long vacation to Australia. He toured all around and loved the outback. He knew that when he started work, he would not be able to afford such an opportunity.

"We're open all the year round and ours is a shop for everyone," he said. "Our style is sporty elegant and I don't succumb to the boutique concept. Customers will find unique items from independent suppliers. For example for women: Brunate, Kennel & Schmenger, Peter Kaiser and Paul Green while the favourite brands for men include Fretz Men and Aldo Bruè. But the special Swiss brand is Kandahar with its unusual features such as its cork insulation, interchangeable wool plush footbed and the three-layer anatomical insole."

Rougemont Interiors

Promenade 3
Tel. 033 7449030
info@rougemontinteriors.com
www.rougemontinteriors.com

In 2013, Pascale Heuberger opened her interior design shop on the Promenade. (See entry, Who's Who). It

Rougemont Interiors.

was a lucky find because the size was ideal, 130m², and as the terrace with its sofas and chairs was an attractive space to socialise, she added a coffee shop.

The shop is a showcase for furniture, fabrics, accessories and gift items. Some of the remarkable objets d'art are in bronze, a metal she likes, and you can also find exquisite fur plaids, Baobab candles, and plenty of little "trouvailles," among many others things. The shop combines a design studio where customised interior projects are created.

"Our ethos is to deliver inspirational interiors so that each client can fulfil his or her dream of the perfect home," said Pascale Heuberger. "Understanding and interpreting both our clients' aesthetic and lifestyle needs is an essential part of our skill set. We therefore can ensure that the design reflects their personality, taste and aspirations. We pride ourselves on designing practical solutions for whatever is required."

Antonella

Promenade 9
Tel. 0337443407
bestcorner.gstaad@ymail.com
www.boutiqueantonella.com

Antonella is the fashion shop where one can find style, quality, good taste and sophisticated fabrics. It also caters to women who are fed up with the big brands and want one of a kind or unique garments. Antonella found

Antonella

the answer in fashions from different cultures like handbags from Venezuela, ponchos from Uruguay, coats from Uzbekistan and dresses from Ukraine. Above all, the aim is for the clothes to be pleasant to wear, ultra comfortable and elegant.

Antonella is renowned for her cashmere collection of jumpers, cardigans, sweaters and stoles which she designs herself. The colours range from subtle to bright rich blues or reds. Some cashmere is embroidered with silk in a special way with twisted needles and others are decorated with chinchilla. The textures vary from plain to thick weaves for the colder weather in Gstaad but the jumpers are still very light.

3

"When I came to Gstaad I discovered my passion on the road of life," said Antonella. "I arrived in 1997 with my husband Fabrizio who is restaurant manager of Lac Retaud and I worked in a shop that I was selling high end quality of cashmere. There I discovered my love of cashmere. I would go to Milan and Paris to see the newest collections and to find new and different styles that I can propose to my clients. After 11 years I opened my own shop on the Promenade in 2008. I only sell the best cashmere from Mongolian sheep."

Antonella grew up in Milan and Genoa where she gained her baccalaureate. Her mother had a fashion shop in Genoa which sold Louis Vuitton bags and women's clothes. She worked in the shop and remembered the first dress she adored. It was red velvet in a A-line which she wore with black patent leather shoes. It goes without saying that fashion is in her DNA.

Marina Anouilh

Showroom
6A Promenade
Tel. 033 744 2042
contact@marinaanouilh.ch
www.marinaanouilh.com

Marina Anouilh runs the Concept Store and it's a enough to say that she has good taste. This is reflected in the cornucopia of colours and things found in this treasure trove of shops within a shop. One of the precious collections that can be found is SEP - a range

Marina Anouilh

of luxury embroidered clutch bags, cushion covers, keffiyeh scarves and shawls handmade by refugee artists living in Jordan. It's contemporary designed products based on traditional Palestinian embroidery and has phenomenal coverage in fashion magazines like Vogue, Harper's Bazaar, the World of Interiors, Elle Decoration, among others. The company is the brainchild of Roberta Ventura, a former banker from Geneva who wanted to provide work for women in the Jerash camp.

"I follow my emotions and usually my feet take me to new accessories from four corners of the world," said Marina, who has the looks of an

English aristocrat, "from the plains of Uzbekistan to the islands of the Aegean Sea, workshops in the cities of the Morocco or India and to Loulou de La Falaise who was Muse of Yves Saint Laurent. I only work with people who inspire me and my suppliers tend to become friends. The human aspect is always at the centre of my selection."

But the Concept Store is mostly about accessories which are an exclamation point to a woman's clothes. Fashionistas agree "...a strong piece of jewellery can make a simple outfit look elegant" (Giorgio Armani). "The perfect accessory can make the difference between looking blah and totally to die for" (Michael Kors). "Accessories are key - nothing beats a cool Panama hat or statement shades - look to Maison Michel or Miu Miu for inspiration." (Poppy Delevingne). "My motto is to go wild on the accessories - the belts, the hair clips, the jewellery." (Heidi Klum).

"I wanted a place that is much more than just a store with pretty things inside," she said. "People feel good here. They chatter and drink tea and I ask questions and they tell me about their lives. It's a place of exchange and discovery as well as a place to shop. It's full of inspirations, cultures and styles. Clothing and accessories include both the exceptional and timeless that we keep all our lives, the little very affordable accessory or original gift that surprises."

Among the shops within a shop are D'ascoli, Rita & Zia, Themis Z and Pink Maharani. D'Ascoli produces fabrics for the home, fashion as well as custom fabrics. The company was started by an American textile designer Peter D'Ascoli who setup a design and product development studio in New Delhi while his wife designs clothes. Rita & Zia was founded by Sandrine Barabinot who is jeweller from Geneva and is known for original and trendy jewellery. While Themis Zouganeli is the designer for a lifestyle brand with a home accessories collection that adds warmth and understated elegance to everyday life and entertainment at home.

Pink Maharani is about the finest cashmere shawls which come from Ladakh at 4,000m and made in a 18-step process from the Capra Hircus goat breed. They are dyed with vegetable colours and woven on a loom. Some of the exquisite shawls are embroidered and take anything from three to nine months to make.

"Now the biggest challenge of all is for me is my e-shop, which is a platform for all these talents and more can join me," she said. "I was astonished recently at my first meeting when different people from diverse places like Afghanistan, Spain, France got on so well - it was like a community. I'm also launching my small exclusive line of clothing."

Marina was born in Geneva of a Greek mother and Italian father. She married the son of the famous French author and playwright, Nicolas Anouilh in 1988 and she delights in spending time at their island home in Kefalonia, Greece. She is an avid reader and one of her favourite authors is Stephan Zweig.

TopPharm Pharmacy

Promenade 44
Tel. 033 748 86 26
apoteke.kropf@gstaad.ch
www.apotheke.ch

The pharmacy's range also includes health products, cosmetics and alternative medicines. The owners, Aldo Kropf and his wife Marianne, are both pharmacists. He is a former politician who was the president of the municipality of Saanen (2009-2015). They are known for their natural wound cream, Riccovitan, and Riccomycin for infected wounds.

"I was born and raised in Basel," he said. "My passion for playing the drums connects me deeply to music in general. However, I enjoy listening intently to the music at the concerts. We came to Gstaad 27 years ago when we bought the chemist and have three children, none of whom will be following in our footsteps. We encourage them to do what they like and let them choose their own profession."

He maintains strong ties with Basel through his support of FC Basel and his Alma Mater, Basel university. He still is a lecturer and teaches Ph.D students as well as supervising internships for them. Kropf is the president of the Gstaad Menuhin Festival.

Cadonau

Promenade 68
Tel. 033 744 12 32
Cadonau-gstaad@bluewin.ch
www.cadonau-gstaad.ch

A bookshop that is more than a bookshop because it has stationery (including art materials and calendars), toys, clothes for the whole family, souvenirs (even dog collars, cuckoo locks and fridge magnets) and it loves kids. It has been an important presence on the Promenade for over 70 years.

During the peak seasons, all sorts of celebrities pop in. For example, Elton John, Claudia Schiffer and the Swedish Princess Madeleine who is friends with Cedric Notz and his wife Andrea. (See entry, Cedric Notz). But what their purchases are, remain secret.

"That's one of the advantages of Gstaad," said Irene Treuthardt, the Manager. "Discretion. No paparazzi. No autograph hunters."

Lorenz Bach

3

Maison Lorenz Bach

Promenade 81
3780 Gstaad
Tel. 033 744 6878

High season: open
from Monday to Sunday.
Low season: open
from Monday to Saturday.

The Lorenz Bach fashion range is not exclusive in the boutique. It is always mixed with other brands so the clients can achieve their own look. (See Who's Who, Lorenz Bach)

Maison Lorenz Bach's story began over 35 years ago as the first high fashion boutique on the elegant promenade of Gstaad. Created by a man of true style with an eye for fashion whose inspiration is drawn from the beauty and colours of the Alps. The boutiques can be found in the most exclusive Swiss ski resorts of Gstaad, Crans-Montana, Zermatt, Verbier and Villars, and sell beautiful selection of clothing from the finest designers. From luxury labels, to more unique and coveted brands.

"You will always find the most chic and beautiful pieces from each collection at our boutiques," said Lorenz. "Our in-house brands Lorenz Bach and Maison LB, reflect our philosophy to provide the upmost in quality, comfort and tailoring."

Urs von Unger

Gstaad-Saanen shops

Urs von Unger

Kleines Landhaus
Dorfstrasse 71
Saanen
Tel. 033 744 4411
mail@ursvonunger.com
www.ursvonunger.com

Urs von Unger is a charming interior decorator who has a natural sense of taste, design and harmony at his fingertips. When it comes to renovation of a old chalet, a grand country house or finding the right modern furniture or antiques for the interior design, he is a expert par excellence. His masterpiece is the historic house, the Kleines Landhaus in Dorfstrasse, Saanen, where he runs an art and antiques gallery.

"In my work I respect the individual personality of my clients as well as the history of the buildings," he said. "My aim is to create a dialogue between things. To get a sense of it you just need to walk around my gallery. My style is eclectic and I mix old and modern. I choose the pieces always by feeling."

Urs was born and educated in Basel. His first position was in a family office before he decided to explore something creative. When he was 27 he opened a flower shop in his house in the Old Town, a house where Jakob Burckhardt, a famous cultural historian of art lived from 1866-1892.

He was an innovative florist and his floral arrangements were a mix of seasonal flowers, greenery and berries from all over Europe. It was during this period where he discovered and appreciated that nature was a great inspiration to art, design and beauty. The annual vernissage for the winter exhibition became a key social event in the Basel calendar.

His success as a florist led to the opening of a second shop in the building of the Basel courthouse next to the Beyeler gallery. Hildy Beyeler who was his neighbour and adored flowers, helped him to get this sought-after space.

"In my early thirties I opened my first antique shop," said Urs. "My first purchase was an 18th century frame which I found on one my travels in the South of France. It started me off on my now collection. I liked old things because they had a story to tell and stimulated my curiosity. It was a natural development because when I was younger I liked diving into other worlds through reading books such as Tolstoy's War and Peace. So I progressed from being an observer to a participant."

He had skied in Gstaad before he came to sell antiques and art during a winter season. As he was pleased with the results, he rented premises. He sold a mixture of Swiss rustic and furniture which included the work of 18th century prominent cabinet makers like atelier Funk. There was always a large choice of mirrors from the 17th to the 19th century. His current pieces include Calyxte Campe, Kris Lamba, McCollin Bryan, Guy de Rougemont, Orsina Sforza, and Manuela Zervudachi as well as a handpicked selection of rustic and elegant antiques.

"At the same time, I had my antique shop, friends asked me to help them with their houses," he said. "So in the off-season, I became an interior decorator by word of mouth and had commissions in Switzerland and abroad. One was a dilapidated farmhouse in Oberbort Gstaad which was built from scratch and only the fence and wood from one room remained. I was lucky and within several months found 200 year old slate tiles, old door handles, etc. My carefully selected furniture include pieces such as monastic chairs and a table from a convent in Switzerland."

The Kleines Landhaus is his "heart piece" and he takes a great pride in it. It was the house of the Bernese bailiff from 1575 to 1665. Urs' work of love was to give this important building its former glory.

"Each corner, each door was carefully restored," he said. "I was most fortunate to find a piece of a 'Speckofen' dated 1613 that was formerly part of the stove in the house. Its insignia was the bear of Bern and the crane of Saanenland. Then after a long search I found a 17th century oven with the perfect dimensions to finally bring the pieces together and place the oven in its original position. One of the modern additions to the house is the wonderful staircase with a brass railing that ascends to the magnificent attic room."

The art and antique gallery is certainly worth a visit not only to enter the inner sanctum of this magnificent building but also to discover the interplay between the beautiful objects inside. A hushed calm presides as a customer moves between the eclectic objects each enriching the other by its presence and releasing a Wow factor for the viewer.

Schmid's Dorflade.

Schmid's Dorflade

The Mini-Market of Saanen Village

Dorfstrasse 76
Saanen
Tel. 033 748 75 74
dorflade@schmid-saanen.ch
www.schmid-saanen.ch

The mini-market is an independent family business run by Walter Schmid, third generation and his daughter Sarah Schmid, fourth generation. It was founded in 1927 by Walter's grandfather Robert in the family's chalet which was built in 1627. Well known for its top quality of fruit and vegetables, the shop has a special room to ensure their freshness. Here you can find varieties of fruit and vegetables often difficult to find or rarely seen.

"I took over the shop from my father, Jakob, with my brother and sister in 1984," he said, "and when I look back over 40 years, I'm proud that we turned it into important regional distribution business. Today, at the other end of Dorfstrasse, Schmid's Fruit, Vegetables and Drinks AG has over 2,000m2 of storage and sorting space, and 12 delivery vans working 365 days a year. In the region of the three lakes - Biel, Murten and Neuchatel, there is the vegetable garden and that's where we buy the highest quality of produce. For fruit we go directly to the Valais which is well known for its top quality."

Walter's sports include tennis, skiing, swimming and curling. He also won the Romandie championship of curling three times. When it comes to choices of food and drink, he opts for fruit which is 50% of his meal intake daily. He drinks espresso and wine in the evening.

Sarah is the opposite and opts for a vegetables even Vegan. Her main sport is horse riding which she began as a child. She and her other two siblings helped in the shop at an early age.

"They were our child labourers," joked her father. "They had to select three qualities of beans out of 50 kgs bag. And Sarah was very good at it."

Sarah was educated at the secondary school OSZ and later gained at diploma at the Ecole supérieure de Commerce, La Neuveville. (See entry, OSZ). In between, she went on a trip to Ontario, Canada where she was introduced to Canadian free range horses which she now rides.

"At La Neuveville, I decided to do a dictionary of fruit and vegetables," she said, "Customers were always asking me questions about vegetables and fruit and what the equivalent names were in different languages. So my dictionary is in five languages. For example, bärlauch (allium ursinum) or wild garlic in English grows in the forest where there's light."

"It can be chopped up finely and put on buttered bread," added Walter. "Its great to eat or is used in different recipes such as a pesto or as a filling in ravioli. But what we both like is asparagus either in a soup or grilled."

Enzian Keramik

Oberdorfstrasse 23
3792 Saanen
Tel. 033 744 2302
enziankeramik@gmx.ch
www.enziankeramik.ch

Pottery is one of the traditional crafts that can be found in Saanen. Christine Baumgartner is a potter who creates her own range of crockery. Her workshop with its kiln that fires clay to 1,100°C is worth a visit because you can see how a piece of clay can create an artwork.

"My inspiration comes from various sources and I also create personalised orders," she said. "One design for espresso cups had a chicken wearing earphones. It was a present for a friend who worked in sound production. Another was to copy a design from a medieval church onto mugs and plates. Since then, I've used the design in different ways to decorate my stoneware."

The pride of place in the workshop is collection of chicken sculptures. They vary in size from large cocks to hens of different sizes and colours. The theme of poultry is also featured on jugs, mugs and plates.

"The chicken sculptures are not my idea but were in inherited from a former colleague who lived on a chicken farm," she said. "They are popular among customers. My speciality is painting on the stoneware and my signature is not to glaze everything. For example, the matt or rough texture gives it a better grip on the handle of a mug and is also an interesting design feature."

Giovanella

Oberdorfstrasse 15
3792 Saanen
Tel. 0337442526
giovalux@bluewin.ch
www.giovanella.ch

Today, when one thinks of glass, Murano comes to mind. Saanen too has its glass artist, Isabelle Giovanella. She is the third generation to have a workshop for stained glass windows. Besides restoring centuries-old windows in churches, she makes stained glass lamps, wall lamps, exterior glass lamps as well as speciality windows which are a popular feature of chalets and luxurious chalets in Gstaad. Roundel glass is mostly favoured but for a stylish look, rose glass with specks of gold is an alternative. It similar to the aventurine glass also known as goldstone glass which was discovered in Murano in the early 15th century and is brownish translucent with copper specks.

"Glass making has not changed a lot over the centuries," said Isabelle. "In 1120, Theophilus Presbyter, a German Benedictine monk wrote a book called Diverse Arts which included a section on producing stained glass and the techniques of glass painting. One ingredient used in the paint was wine

Isabelle Giovanella

or urine. Maybe when they finished the wine, they used the urine."
The range of coloured glass is huge and some 5,000 are available. Besides its use in lamps, two sheets can be fused together to create doors or can be shaped into different forms.

"One of the satisfying jobs I did, was the Anglican church of St Peter's in Chateau d'Oex," she said. "I restored all windows and for example, cleaned others which were thick with blackened wax from candles. Another job was to paint the glass with scenes from early periods to today at the restaurant hotel Bären in Gsteig which was built in the 17th century."
She recommends a visit to the

Monastery Königsfelden in Windisch, Aargau because the coloured stained glass windows are the most beautiful in Switzerland. The church and the double monastery were built as a memorial in 1308 by the widow of the murdered King Albrecht I von Habsburg.

Isabelle is a talented glass artist whose studio is located in a 19th century building. She has experience of designing windows and lamps from Gothic to Art Nouveau and Contemporary styles. She also likes to undertake special commissions of designs as well as glass fusing, glass collages and creating one of a kind glass lamps for clients.

Intercoiffure Marti

Dorfstrass 67
Tel 033 744 11 47
info@intercoiffure-marti.ch
www.intercoiffure.ch

The salon is modern and stylish with a light and airy ambience. It has a team of five stylists with a diverse range of products and treatments that include L'Oréal Paris, Gerda Spillman and Kératase Paris. The salon is also a member of the Intercoiffure Mondial and Suisse which enables it to be ahead of the fashion trends in hairdressing. It's owned by Heinz Marti who is a stylist for both men's and women's hair, and his wife, Begoña Garcia.

"In the digital age of Facebook and Instagram," said Begoña, "everyone can see the latest hairstyles on internet and show us what they want. However, as professionals we can also advise them what is best for their face shape and hair type."

"My aim in the salon is to make the clients feel comfortable whether they are a celebrity, a local or a visitor," said Heinz. "As you know the slogan of Gstaad is come up and slow down. Well ours is come in, sit down and relax. We've a good team spirit and one thing we don't allow is to let the phone ring more than three times. It's most annoying to customers to wait to make an appointment."

An outstanding feature of the salon are the windows which are decorated by Begoña. She has a natural talent for the displays which attracts many passers-by.

Heinz was born in Saanen and remembers how once all the cars passed through the village. Later, it was pedestrianised which added charm to the place with its medieval houses and streets. (See entry, Benz Hauswirth).

"For me the biggest compliment from customer is when she smiles as she leaves the salon," said Begoña Garcia, a third generation Saner as her grandfather came from Spain.

Zwahlen-Hueni

Dorfstrasse 50/52
3792 Saanen
Tel. 033 744 16 87
info@zwahlenhueni.ch
www.zwahlenhueni.ch

Le Tresor

Promenade 65
Tel. 033 744 0180
info@zwahlenhueni.ch
www.zwahlenhueni.ch

Zwahlen-Hueni is a haute couture brand with fashion shops which played an important role in the Saanenland for over 70 years. A new chapter started in 2019 when Philipp Zwahlen, the son of Alexander and Simone took over the business. At the core of their range is the janker, a traditional Austrian or Bavarian costume. It's a waist-length jacket with a stand-up collar, made of boiled wool or linen, which can be dyed in different colors such as grey, green or red. The buttons of this jacket are usually made of metal or horn. The fabric edges can be made of a different colour.

"Today the janker has totally modernised," said Philipp Zwahlen, the third generation. "If you look around at our choice, you will find the fashionable styles which for women can be cheeky and chic. A good made-to-measure janker which is fitted in our atelier can be worn instead of a traditional jacket or a tuxedo. It's trendy nowadays for both men and women to wear them with jeans or chinos."

One thing that astonishes a client when they enter the store is the blaze of different colours like the cashmere pullovers. The variety of brands for men, women and children range from Vicomte A, from Paris; Lieblingsstück newly interpreted jankers which are one-offs; Marco Polo for women,; Susanne Spatt from Salzburg with her beautiful designs; Longchamp handbags; stylish Poldi jankers from Munich; Zapf hats with capes to match; Gran Sasso from Italy; Woolrich and Barbour; Doriani cashmere from Milan which is synonymous with male elegance; and Crockett & Jones shoes.

"It was natural that I would continue in my parents' footsteps as I knew the business so well," said Philipp a handsome chap in his early 20's. "When I was a boy, I even went on buying trips with them to Zurich and Salzburg. I also came to have lunch with my grandparents who lived above the shop and was given my favourite dishes.

Like his father, Philipp studied at the textile college in Zurich and obtained a bachelor in textile business management. Consequently, he has good understanding of fabrics. His textile brands include Daks of London and he recommends the use of cashmere or herringbone for the jankers. He is proud of his heritage and that the metal buttons for jackets reflect the Zwahlen coat of arms - a rampant alpine ibex. But above all, he has a bachelor pad above the shop.

Drogerie Jaggi.

Drogerie Jaggi

Dorfstrasse 54
3792 Saanen
Tel. 033 744 1321

The Drogerie Jaggi has comprehensive range of natural remedies, health products, cosmetics and veterinary medicines. The natural remedies include the familiar Homeopathy and the Bach Flower as well as three other remedies which are not as well known. Spagyrik essences which are sprayed in the mouth and then rubbed in on the arms are among the most effective and most useful herbal medicines. They have proved themselves in acute as well as chronic diseases. Schüssler, named after a German doctor, is based on a disruption of the mineral balance. Its mineral salt therapy is simple, risk-free and for every applicable healing method. Spenglersan are microbiological medicines that can strengthen your immune system and your overall constitution. The immune system is a defence against bacteria and viruses and against the toxins produced by these pathogens. Ceres is a tincture which is drunk neat or with water. It is gentle remedy of low dosage, high quality manufacturing that can be taken with other natural remedies.

"I'm a muesli man," said Peter Jaggi, the third generation who is athletic and fit, "except sometimes when I have breakfast with my little kids. I mix various ingredients obviously avoiding sugar and adding millet which is good for hair. I'm pleased that I can offer such a wide range of products to the locals who are generally healthy except for chronic rheumatism or other minor illnesses. But then we have natural remedies to treat them."

Peter was born in Saanen and studied at the same Neuchatel school as his grandfather, Werner and father, Niklaus. He is proud of the way the drogerie has developed throughout the generations. He remembered as boy that his grandfather would receive products in bulk and how they were decanted into small bottles. He and his father, gradually extended the shop and today it has an optimum space. In 1987, he founded another drogerie in Lenk. and runs both.

Blumen Stricker

Kirchgasse 6
Saanen
Tel. 033 748 62 72
info@blumenstricker.ch
www.blumentricker.ch

Andi Stricker is a self made man and a gardener par excellence. He runs two big garden centres in Saanen and Zweisimmen with a range of flowers and plants that would thrill anyone who loves flowers. One may well ask what is his favourite flower or plant? The saffron crocus which is more valuable than gold or the Juliet Rose that sold for millions? No, the ariocarpus or flowering cactus. He has over 2,000 of them at his home in Schönried. They are low maintenance as they are watered every two weeks and flower once a year.

"Our core business is selling flowers and plants as well as providing services such as annual contracts for looking after gardens, winter decorations and tending to flower boxes," he said. "The most popular indoor plants are phalaenopsis orchids while the outdoor plants are petunias or geraniums that fill the thousands of window boxes and are low maintenance as they're connected to the Blumat automatic watering system. Chalet owners say,'look at my beautiful flowers."

The garden centre is Saanen has a selection of houseplants, seasonal plants, perennials, woody plants, fruit and berries, fertilisers, plant protection, planters, garden products, floristry, cut flowers and floral decorations. The choice in any of the categories is large and one can easily spend a whole morning or afternoon there.

Andi was born in Saanen and he followed in the footsteps of his father who was a gardener. He was diligent in his studies and after his apprenticeship in St Gallen, Aargau, among other places, he obtained a diploma as chief gardener. At the age of 24, he gained the final diploma that enabled him to manage or run his own business. In 1994, he agreed to take over his father's business which was on the same site as the garden centre today. But it was a small concern and on the land owned by the municipality.

"My father had a bad deal with the gemeinde as he could be given short notice to move in three months," he said. "I knew what I wanted and told them if they couldn't give it to me I'd go somewhere else. Consequently, I renegotiated the contract to lease the land for 35 years. I have 2,500m2 which includes 900m2 sales area spread over three floors and 600 m2 outdoor area. The rest is storage and equipment space. It's a true plant wonderland including garden decorations such as Buddha statues which is the latest trend among the young customers."

At one stage in his life he was a mountain climber and went on trips to the Valais with friends to climb the 4,000m peaks. On one occasion his friends brought along Lucia who became his future wife. They have a child, Nicola.

The staff normally has coffee at 9am and years ago, Andi recalled that they talked to each other about all sorts of things. Now everybody sits in silence communicating with others on WhatsApp.

"I think that the smartphone is a real disrupter of society," said Andi. "Sometimes I feel like just stamping on it. I need it for business and only spend an hour on it which is too much."

"Photography is an important part of my life and I go on photographic trips to various countries," he said. "I normally dislike buildings in my pictures but there are exceptions like the chalets in Saanenland which add to the beauty of the landscape. I found the same in the Lofoten islands in Norway where the red fisherman's cottages were part of the beautiful seascape."

La Scarpa51

Dorfstrasse 51
3792 Saanen
Tel. 033 855 5151
lascarpa51@bluewin.ch

La scarpa (Italian for shoe) is a real discovery. It's different from other shoe shops. The reason is that it's run by Gabrielle Gagneux who adds her artistic touch to the shoes she stocks. So you will get her version of a slipper, a ballet or court shoe. It will be a little detail like a different colour or fabric to a ballet shoe or to the standard Alexa with a 5cm block heel. Through her personal touch she creates something chic or elegant for both women and men. With her background in Hermes and Loro Piana she has impeccable taste.

"Accessories refresh and renew outfits," she said. "In a stroke a woman looks fashionable again. It can be a matter of a scarf, a pair of gloves, a handbag, shoes or a matching handbag and shoes. Most people have trouble with shoes. I had big feet as a child and my problem started when I tried to

Blumen Stricker.

Gabrielle Gagneux

squeeze them into smaller shoes." Gabrielle was born in Gstaad, grew up in Aargau and graduated from the commercial school in La Neuveville and the Ecole hôtelière de Lausanne (EHL). Her work experience included cruise ships, a pharmaceutical company, a conference centre but mostly big fashion brands.

"My dream was to have my own shop in Saanen," she said. "When my brother-in-law, Alexander Zwahlen told me that there was a vacant place, I snapped it up. As his son, Philipp, my nephew, runs the Zwahlen-Hüni shops, I choose suede leather for my shoes to match the janker clothing." (See entry, Zwahlen-Hueni).

Among the unusual items in the shop are the Candice Cooper lace up boots for men which have zips along the sides and feet slip in them like moccasins. Another is the natural boots made out of boiled wool that keep the feet warm even in temperatures of -35°C. They come with lanolin insoles.

Gstaad-Schönried Shops

Chnusper-Becke

Dorfstrasse 32
3778 Schönried
Tel. 033 744 1484
info@chnusper-becke.ch
(See Chapter 2. Bakers)

Buure Metzg

Gstaad-Schönried
Dorfstrasse 64
3778 Schönried
Tel. 0337441939
www.buuremetzg.ch

When customers step in here they are in another world of butchers. Some say it's a gourmet's paradise. Martin Hauswirth, the owner, offers a wide assortment you never expect to find: fish, fruit, vegetables and pan-ready or a traiteur assortment. Then there's the pièce de résistance, the meat. The selection varies from bone-aged meat (côte de bœuf, T-bone, entrecôte), homemade (raw ham, coppa, mostbröckli, bacon, sausage pies and terrines), charcuterie (cold cuts, Buureschinken, dry sausage, salami) and pre-cooked dishes which can be heated at home as well as cold prepared plates (pâtés / terrines, antipasti, salads and apèro finger food).

"Our butcher shop is unique," said Martin Hauswirth. "It's a one-stop shop. My team includes my wife, Nicole, who supervises all the non-meat products and runs the administration."

Martin Hauswirth whose father was a farmer was born in Gstaad and served an apprenticeship with Ruedi Matti. Martin has been a butcher for almost 40 years and is proud of his profession.

"With our branches in Gstaad and Schönried, we're the only butchers in Saanenland and use only local meat," he said, "because we know where it comes from and even in some cases the name of the cow. The exceptions are at peak times when entrecôte and fillet have to be bought from Emmental. Our hits are bone matured meat, dried raw ham, coppa, dried meat, bacon and mostbröckli. They are prepared in a special drying room in Lauenen by Rolf von Siebenthal until they have reached an ideal consistency and taste and have won several gold medals by the Swiss Meat Federation." (See Robert Bratschi, Buure Metzg Gstaad)

"You don't become a butcher unless you have a passion because you work hard, sometimes for 11 hours," he said. "We're up at 5am and open at 6am. I'm proud and grateful that all the hotels and restaurants are good customers which is a recognition of their appreciation of high quality. My favourite meat is entrecôte steak. For relaxation, I ski, ride my mountain bike and go hunting. We have young son, Niklas, and I hope one day, he will follow in my footsteps as a butcher."

Chapter 4. Accommodation

4

Finest selection of hotels in Canton Bern: from family run luxury to cosy, comfortable and beds in the oldest beautiful chalet.

Room at The Alpina

The Alpina Gstaad

Alpinastrasse 23
Tel. 033 888 9888
info@thealpinagstaad.ch
www.thealpinagstaad.ch

The Alpina Gstaad which is known by the locals as the James Bond hotel is the first 5-star superior to be built in the resort for over a century. No expense was spared in building the hotel by the owners Jean-Claude Mimran and Marcel Bach. Since it opened, the hotel has won many accolades by the media from TripAdvisor to Bilanz, Tatler and Travel + Leisure.

The luxury boutique hotel of 56 bedrooms and suites is iconic through its refinement and Alpine chic. It features natural materials like marble, sandstone and aged wood and brims over with facilities usually associated with big hotels. The multifaceted Six Senses Spa includes a healing grotto with bricks of pink Himalayan salt next to the saunas and steam rooms. Complimentary fitness classes are offered daily. The outdoor pool is the resort's centre in the summer and the indoor pool in the winter. A special feature is the contemporary art collection.

"Art has been a passion of mine since I was very young," said Nachson Mimran, Chairman of the Board of Directors. "As the hotel was taking shape, we thought about creating a cultural ethos for The Alpina Gstaad. Our guests certainly seem to enjoy being surrounded by art. Today the emphasis is sustainability throughout the property. Tim Weiland, the General Manager shares our vision of sustainable luxury, brings international experience in the luxury hotel industry and is accustomed to recognising and fulfilling the needs of our international guests."

The James Bond touches include

the subterranean drive that swoops through a cavern of brown Ringgenberg limestone and skirts a frozen waterfall before snaking up to a glamorous carriage entrance; the shadowy light that comes on automatically in the bathroom as a guest enters in the dead of night - enough to show the way but not enough to wake anybody; the cigar lounge which is a pre-Castro replica because Marcel Bach who is an aficionado of cigars wanted his guests to smoke in an authentic atmosphere. (See entry, Macel Bach).

In addition, there's a 14-seat private cinema with a popcorn machine, two Michelin starred restaurants including a Japanese restaurant and the show-stopper Panoramic suite which is a duplex penthouse with its cathedral ceiling spa and sculptural fireplace.

Tim Weiland is perfect for Gstaad. He values discretion most highly in a resort where that quality is greatly appreciated. Most of his experience has been in small luxury hotels and consequently, he is very hands-on. He makes sure to welcome guests on arrival and to be present on departure.

"Some of my memorable experiences include organising events for A-listers," he said in an engaging manner, "where no one would have known they existed. A wedding took place where there were kilos of magnificent flowers and a vast wedding cake that weighed 100 kilos. It was kept intimate and a total secret to the outside. Another event in Morocco included a 1,000 lanterns with candles and staff went around to replace candles that had burnt out."

He grew up in Cape Town and gained his BA in hospitality at Ecole hôtelière de Lausanne (EHL). Prior to joining the Alpina, he was at the Aman Le Mélézin in Courchevel. His previous experiences over the last 10 years was with the Aman Group that took him to exotic destinations from the Maldives to Thailand, to Marrakech, Rajasthan in India and Beijing.

"Throughout my career, I have lived amongst different cultures from Muslim, Hindu and atheist," he said. "My philosophy is first to listen, learn and understand."

Martin Göschel is the Michelin-starred head chef who presides over the three restaurants at the Five-star boutique hotel Alpina. There is the Japanese Megu, the Swiss Stubli and Sommet, a showcase for Martin's culinary talents which he describes as modern Mediterranean cuisine. But he excels in surprising guests with his visual and taste-intensive dishes. There are various amuse bouches for example, the yellow egg yolk with caviar in the form of a small, crispy sandwich. It looked delicious but my companion hesitated as she could imagine the runny yolk doing its damage. But it proved otherwise as it's solid and has the texture of a marshmallow. The secret according to Martin was slow cooking. Another original amuse bouche was the carpaggio of lobster - thin slices with caviar and a subtle marinade.

The first course on the 'Signature Menu' are sole rolls with herbs on puntarelle salad in saffron sauce. There, the luxurious saffron taste is mixed with dried tomatoes. But an alternative for Veggies is the vegetable roll with puntarelle salad in a saffron sauce. Another delight both visual and for taste is the red beetroot goat cheese macaron. Here the mix is of a little sweetness and subtle earthiness. But the scallops take the first prize: they are served with a chartreuse of asparagus and Perigord truffle stuffed with riesling white sauce. Or ravioli in thin dough or risotto of scalop served in its shell.

Meat is also an important part of the menu. There is Simmental veal fillet wrapped in seaweed or sliced and served with medallions of oxtail. The alternative is the fillet steak, tender with a spicy flavour.

The desserts again rise to the occasion. The white chocolate balls which conceal lime sorbet is exquisite and there is the popular moelleux au chocolat with crystallised kumquats and oranges.

Great service from a dedicated team. In summer, guests can chill by the pool and the Sommet menu can be served on the terrace.

"In the future, The Alpina Hotel will also become a platform for progressive forward thinkers," said Nachson Mimran. "A lab intersecting science and technology with emphasis on the social environment impact."

Gstaad Palace

Palacestrasse 28
Tel. 033 748 50 00
info@palace.ch
www.palace.ch

The Gstaad Palace hotel which is perched over the village like a fairytale castle is its undisputed social centre. Photos on its walls of visitors including stars (Elizabeth Taylor, Richard Burton, Sophie Loren, Roger Moore), politicians (Margaret Thatcher, President Jimmy Carter, President Jacques Chirac, Kofi Annan), musicians (Elton John, Paul McCartney, Diana Ross) bear testament to its enduring appeal to the rich and famous and as well as the discreet and monied.

When the GreenGo discotheque — Gstaad's first real nightclub, opened over 45 years ago, it was an overnight hit. They sold some 50 steak tartares from 4 am to 7am. The club's dance floor sits over an indoor pool, and revellers often ended up skinny-dipping. GreenGo has attracted everyone from Princess Diana to a lip-syncing Tina Turner and Madonna and her daughter Lourdes. But it was so beloved by Peter Sellers and filmmaker Blake Edwards that they filmed part of the 1975 The Return of the Pink Panther there. One

Andrea Scherz

of the most coveted tickets in town (from CHF 1,250) is the Palace's New Year's Eve party, a bacchanalian affair flowing in caviar and champagne that's known for impromptu performances - John Travolto and Bono have been among those who sung 'off the cuff' songs.

For some A-listers, a stay at the Palace is just as a good a reason to visit Gstaad rather than hitting the slopes. They come to hide away and treat the hotel as their winter clubhouse. The time to come is the Christmas high season when the VIPs and multimillionaires descend on the village to celebrate. However, there is a need to book a couple of years ahead. The staff swells from 50 to 300 and work some 13-hour days to fulfil the demanding requests of the guests in the 104 rooms. Over the years, they have varied from feeding a cat of a French aristocrat caviar to flying-in a singer to perform in front of a guest for less than a hour. But above all, the place is 'a home away from home' as the staff know your favourite table in the restaurant, that you like a Tom Collins served in a Collins glass over ice or your lunch menu for dining on the glacier.

"We're used to pampering our guests and our loyal staff who've been with us for decades are masters at cosseting them," said Andrea Scherz, scion of the dynasty who've owned it since 1938. "They know the likes and dislikes of each of the regulars. And Palace guests never get no for an answer. The worst scenario is an alternative. Once we had a request from an American who attended the winter Olympics at Albertville (France), about 80km from Gstaad. He was rather short and asked us to raise the height of the floor in his suite as his panoramic view from the armchair was obscured by railings on the balcony. The carpenter carried out his request and increased the height by 60cm."

A original experience is to live like an 18th century farmer in the Walig hut (1,700m). Although the hut has been modernised, it has a log fire for warmth, a wood-burning stove to boil a pan of water for morning coffee and an outside lavatory. But it does include on arrival a sumptuous three-course meal with Swiss red or white wine. The guests have a choice of a chef cooking the meal or as it is pre-prepared the husband and wife can join in a team-building experience by cooking it themselves. The Walig Hut is the brainchild of Andrea Scherz, who is the third generation of his family to run the Gstaad Palace. His father Ernst was responsible for the indoor swimming pool, extending the restaurant terrace, adding the squash court and two apartment blocks.

"We're open for six months of the year," he said. "About three months in the winter and three months in the summer. I'm proud that we are still run by the family - there only three other 5-star hotels in Switzerland that are family run. I took over the hotel from my father in 1996 first to run the rooms division and then as General Manager in 2001. I studied at Ecole hôtelière de Lausanne (EHL) and worked at other 5-stars such as the Beau-Rivage in Lausanne, Savoy in London and the Halekulani in Hawaii."

There are four fine dining options available. It varies from the smart and intimate Le Grill where the speciality is Simmental veal with mushrooms, Gildo's the Italian restaurant where fresh pasta can be cooked at the table to the La Fromagerie, the traditional Swiss chalet restaurant where you can enjoy the speciality of champagne and truffle fondue. (Originally used as a vault to store Swiss gold during the Second World War and hence the heavy original armoured door). The lobby bar is the heart of the hotel, a cozy place where guests come to be seen or can indulge in serious people-watching over fish and chips or a hamburger. It's not unusual to find the bar heaving with people at midnight. Last but not least, the team that makes the dining experience unique from Franz Faeh, culinary director and the maîtres d'Hôtel are Andrea Buschini and Simone Tosin. The sommerliers are Andrea Maffei and Sylvain Herpe and Vittorio di Carlo is vice director.

Andrea Scherz won the Hotelier of the Year 2019 which is awarded by Karl Wild, journalist and hotel tester. The hotel which opened in 1913, got traction from the mountain railway Montreux Berner Oberland Bahn (MOB) railway which extended to Gstaad in 1904-1905.

HUUS Hotel

Schönriedstrasse 74
Gstaad-Saanen
Tel. 0337480404
welcome@huusgstaad.com
www.huusgstaad.com

When is a hotel more than a hotel? When it's a HUUS, the Swiss German word for home and welcomes you as a good friend whether you are a family with children, a businessman, a hiker or biker, a young couple or an old couple. It has a big heart and likes to bring people together and anticipate their

4

needs. The hosts behind the innovative concept are Mirka Czybik (General Manager) and Günter Weilguni (CEO). They focus on taste, comfort and adventure.

"Our lobby looks like a living room and guests will find something like a sofa, chair or a book," said Mirka a charming hotelier, "to make them feel comfortable and at home. Then they can relax in our 1,500m² spa area and if they want adventure there are add-ons like guided winter hikes, mountain biking and rafting. The third element is taste and the head chef Giuseppe Colella takes care of guests appetites. The most important thing is that people must feel at home and the hotel encourages that through the fact that there are no doors anywhere as it's open plan everywhere."

On seven floors the classic Alpine chalet overlooks Saanen and Gstaad and covers almost 10,000m2. Each space of this traditional chalet has been designed through the removal of walls and the enlargement of windows to expose the region's grandeur and natural beauty while settling guests in a home-like surroundings. The use of beautiful wood, fabrics, rocks and ropes (all locally sourced) constantly remind you of the Swiss Alps. Although the largest hotel in the region with 136 rooms and suites, the communal fireplace and library with 500 books engender cosiness and an inviting atmosphere. The Swedish architectural firm Stylt Trampoli have succeeded admirably with the mixture of Nordic influences and alpine traditions.

"The hotel is popular with conferences as we have a choice of seven meeting rooms from 37m2 to 128m2," said Mirka. "They are bright and interconnected. At the other end, HUUS goes the extra mile for kids with a special kids breakfast buffet, kids eating areas that is open all day, kids only spa and kids play rooms adapted to their age. Also a games/cinema room for younger ones and a huge games area (consoles, TV's, pool tables etc.) for the older ones."

Mirka, is a hospitality professional with a bachelor degree from Germany and Cornell university's good manufacturing practice diploma. She has had varied experience in hotels from the large German chain, Steigenberger (2004-2009) to the hotel Alpine Lodge (2009-2015) and joined HUUS in 2015. For most of her career, she has worked alongside Günter Weilguni and when he asked her to join HUUS which was a major challenge, she did not hesitate. Her philosophy is simple, "go for it!"

"I knew I wanted to be a hotelier since I was a young boy," said Günter Weilguni who is a native of the Tyrol and a Swiss national. "When together with Marwan Naja we bought the building for launching HUUS, I had the opportunity of introducing innovative ideas. I wanted a hotel for three generations which also has a lot to offer seminar guests. So I combined these categories with free add-ons such as off-piste skiing in winter, guided hikes and river rafting in summer including equipment. The result was our occupancy rates in winter rose to a high of 92%. Another factor was to classify the hotel as a four star superior because I not only wanted to satisfy the guests but exceed their expectations."

"I never thought I would be a hotelier," said Marwan Naja, who was Beirut born and a financier in Geneva. "Günter came up with the concept that appealed to me. I had some suggestions such as the hotel's terrace and high-tech services which were incorporated. My role is to build on the concept and see us focused to make sure that this ends up as a successful investment."

The menu of the main restaurant is a showcase for Giuseppe Colella's simple Mediterranean cuisine. Starters vary from a pot of aubergine and parmigiana to tuna carpaccio with ginger and carpaccio. A highlight is calamari stuffed with shrimps olives and capers on crunchy bread and salty tomatoes.

The mains include the delicious lamb sirloin pieces served with a purée of vitelotte potatoes and miniature broccoli. Traditional pasta is a signature dish and Giuseppe offers guests the option of any sauce or even making their own. Fish is a favourite and a diverse choice is available. Slightly smoked perch with lavender/saffron sauce and crunchy vegetables is contrasted with sole meunière, panfried octopus and salmon fillet with fennel salad.

Le Grand Bellevue

Untergstaadstrasse 17
Tel. 033 748 0000
info@bellevue-gstaad.ch
www.bellevue-gstaad.ch

The luxury 5-star superior hotel is located in a park in the centre of Gstaad. But its concept of luxury is based on guests who are passionate about life. There's a private cinema, a Swiss mountain cabin in the grounds for private dining, a ride from the station in Roger Moore's former vintage Bentley, outstanding public areas with customised contemporary furniture (George Smith armchairs), a 17m Chesterfield in the Art Deco bar, a special playroom for kids and at the peak of the season, Krug is offered by the glass. This is besides a 3000m2 spa with an indoor pool and two Michelin starred restaurants, Leonards and the Chesery. Who needs to go to the slopes?

There are 57 elegant bedrooms, of which nine are sophisticated suites and a decor that heralds a new era of Gstaad chic with views across mountains or private parklands. The bathrooms are stocked with Bamford bath products which are driven by a spirit of holistic living and sustainable luxury.

But innovation doesn't only extend to the spa but to the breakfasts where they introduced two new versions of Egg Benedictine - Florentine version with spinach and Norwegian smoked salmon. For the rest, it's fulfilling requests for guests for which all the staff cooperate together to ensure a good stay. A regular guest, for example, wants the mattress changed to a softer variety whenever they come.

Daniel Koetser, the owner and Managing Director, is an old Etonian who gained a degree at Glion Hospitality Management School. His father, David Koetser is the prominent art dealer in Old Masters who was one of the founders of the TEFAF. (See entry, David Koetser). Daniel married Davia, the daughter of Rudolf Maag, the Swiss billionaire who has chalets in Gstaad.

Hotel Arc-en-ciel

Egglistrasse 24
Tel. 033 7484343
info@arc-en-ciel.ch
www.arc-en-ciel.ch

The Arc-en-ciel is a family-friendly hotel run by the second generation, Christiane Matti. It's a 4-star chalet with 33 spacious rooms and six apartments, all with their own balconies and terraces. Located in a quiet and sunny position with a view of the mountains, it's a ski-in and ski-out hotel next to the cable cars. Open all year round, it was established by her parents, Heinrich and Micheline in 1960.

"I feel privileged as my 94 year old mother still lunches with me every day," she said, "and as she was always a stickler for details always manages to find some thing that needs attention - 'there's too little water for the flowers or today the vegetables not cooked enough.' Hospitality in our family is very much a woman's job and I started at the age five standing on a chair to wash dishes."

After her commercial diploma, she learnt English in Cambridge and studied at the École hôtelière de Lausanne (EHL). Her first job was as an assistant to the manager at 4-star hotel in Lausanne. Later, she returned when her father was ill and has stayed ever since. At one period, her older brother joined and the family worked together as a team for 16 years.

"I took over the hotel some 20 years ago and soon my daughter Amina will join me," she said. "I'm proud that I still have some staff who were hired by my parents and we're one big family. They know the regular guests and their likes. We also have longstanding guests, some are even third generation."

The hotel goes out of its way to please their guests. There are free bicycles, heated outdoor pool in summer, games room, a playground with electric cars for children and a private spa. A ski shop and beauty boutique are across the street.

"My philosophy is to live your dream,"

Hotel Arc-en-ciel.

she said. "Mine is to do with people. Every day is something else. It makes me happy to make other people happy. We even have a love room for romantic couples which features a red heart on the bed."

Hotel Kernen

Dorfstrasse 58
CH-3778 Schoenried
Tel 033 748 4020
info@hotel-kernen.ch
www.hotel-kernen.ch

Hotel Kernen is a charming chalet-style 3-star and is located in Schoenried on the sunny terrace above Gstaad. It has 22 rooms including two junior suites and has been in the same family for some 100 years. The spa and swimming pool facilities of the nearby 5-star Ermitage can be used at a special rate and an 18 hole golf course is a ten minute drive from the hotel.

The Kernen hotel has several unique features. It's open all year round, it's a place for rest and recreation and is run by one of friendliest hoteliers in Gstaad, Bruno Kernen. He is the fourth generation and is a typical story of a local boy who makes good. He was once a downhill world ski champion and today is a one of the top hoteliers in Gstaad.

"I was taught to ski at the age of two," said Bruno, an affable man. "My mother

Bruno Kernen

Olga who manages the hotel with me put me on skis and I skied up and down a snow hill in front of the house. When I was 9 and the only son, my father told me that one day I'll take over the hotel. When I was 13, he told me that he'd found a place for me to learn cooking. I was shocked because while other children were having fun skiing over the weekends, I would be working. At the time was I was keen skier and his decision was a blow to me."

Kernen participated in the Alpine Ski World Cup International competition between 1978 when he won the bronze in the combination and 1989. In the course of his career, he raced 22 times in the top ten. The biggest success was in 1983 when he won the Hahnenkamm race in Kitzbühel. It's considered the most spectacular ski run anywhere and requires the best ski athletes in the world to tackle almost everything. From jumps up to 80m, steep slopes up to 85% gradient, speeds up to 140 km/hr to the 860m height difference from the starting gate (1,665m) to the finish (805m).

"I had a passion for skiing and thought about the sport the moment I woke up to the moment I went to sleep," he said. "I was participating in downhill races and was being trained by the coaches of the Swiss National Team. In 1981, I had a bad fall and hurt my knee.

The meniscus was ripped but not the tendons. After three months when I felt better, I approached the coaches but they were not interested. I trained on my own and through determination made a comeback. Then I was invited back onto the Swiss National Team."

He ended his career in professional skiing in 1989 at the age of 26 after he had not qualified to participate in the World Championship in Vail. He married the same year. But soon he began a second career, studied hospitality in Bern and in 1993, took over the hotel from his parents. In 2017, Hotel Kernen was awarded 7th place in the best 3-star winter hotels in Switzerland by the Tages Anzeiger. Golf, where he has a handicap of 6, has filled the void left by skiing. Both sports induce one to play against oneself. With skiing the enemy is the slope and with golf the enemy is the course.

"My motto as a hotelier is that every client is king and every king is only a client," he said with a smile. "I'm proud of our long tradition of hospitality. We try to exceed the expectations of our clients through our combination of friendly service, rustic elegance and range of outdoor activities. Besides our gourmet menu, I offer game which I hunt myself. The wild animals include chamois, boar, ibex, red and roe deer."

Alpenrose Hotel and Restaurant

Dorfstrasse 14
3778 Schönried
Tel. 0337489191
info@hotelalpenrose.ch
www.hotelalpenrose.ch

The Alpenrose is a family run hotel with 20 rooms and suites. However, it is better known for its gourmet restaurant Azalée which has thrilled palates for over thirty decades. However, they also have another restaurant, Sammy's Grill and Bar which is only open in Winter.

Michel and Carole von Siebenthal are the third generation and have three daughters: Antina who is an artist and whose paintings hang throughout the hotel, Yasmin who assists her parents and Chantal. A warm welcome is given on arrival at the four-star chalet hotel where the ambiance is quiet and friendly. The rooms are south-facing with sunny balconies and great views of the mountains and glaciers.

"We are quite natural people, down to earth and quite discrete," said Carole, an affable and charming woman. "We have many repeat guests and some count the days until their next visit. It's very relaxing here and if they come in winter, they book one of the six open fireplaces. Others go for the rooms with balcony gardens. One of our unique features is that we have flexible rooms. For a start, all are double and many are interconnecting."

Carole comes from Rohrschach on Lake Constance where her father was an architect and her grandmother had a restaurant. She studied administration at the commercial school, St Gallen. Later, she met Michel at Vaduz, Liechtenstein while working in hospitality. They both worked at the famous Real restaurant run by the legendary Felix Real where Michel was a chef. They met young, she was 19 and he, 20, at the moment his father died. They married in 1988 and decided to work as a married couple. They would help his mother Monika in winter and later made the decision to take over Alpenrose.

"One of the decisions we made was to continue the tradition of a gourmet restaurant," she said. "Michel is a passionate cook and liked working with his hands which means he does all the repairs in the hotel. We renovated the hotel and built the extension in 1989. One of the things our guests like is that we are happy to accommodate their needs. We've had a request to look after hamster while a family skied. Some Middle Eastern guests are accommodated when they expect breakfast at noon and dinner at 10pm."

The Azalée menu has a great variety while Sammy's Grill offers grilled crispy chicken, fondues and Italian delicacies. Alpenrose hotel and restaurant

There are surprises too as the von Siebenthals have an electric car charger in the garage as well as their 1957 MG

Carole von Siebenthal

which is used once a year for the old-timer rally which they organise. Carole's hobby involves providing new objet d'art throughout the hotel for which she has a talent.

Sporthotel Victoria

Promenade 72
Tel. 033 7484422
info@victoria-gstaad.ch
www.victoria-gstaad

Tommy Oehrli is the third generation of hoteliers who manages the family hotel. It has a three star rating with 34 rooms including seven singles and the remainder are double and superior rooms. The location is central, right on

Sporthotel Victoria.

the Promenade. Added benefits are the full breakfast included in the rate and a sauna and fitness room. Its restaurant is popular with the locals and standard Swiss dishes such as fondue, roast beef and veal head are served.

"I love keeping up with the tradition of Swiss hospitality," said Tommy, an optimistic and friendly man, "as with the major brands diversity is lost. I enjoy welcoming the grandchildren of our guests whose grandparents met mine and knew my father and mother."

"It's also fun knowing the quirks of some guests. One requested an even number for the room and the floor and was relieved when I gave her No 10 on the second floor."

Tommy is also remarkable man of courage. He had problems with his back and after undergoing an operation, he was told he would never walk again. But he's a stubborn man and through will power he was able to leave his wheelchair and walk again. One of the first things he did was to ski on his favourite mountain, the Videmanette. As he felt strong enough, he kept going until he had done it 26 times in one day as he wanted to set a record. He came third.

"It's amazing how many different people you meet here," he said. "I was a gofer on the movie set for Christmas in Love which starred Danny de Vito. The producer took over the whole Palace hotel for the shooting and one of my duties was to take the film rolls for processing to Geneva. One of the memorable moments was playing poker with Danny which was great fun. Another as when my dad was in hospital and I took the most income during that week which was the world beach volley ball championship."

He was educated at the OSZ where he was teased and called mustard after the Thomy mustard. (See entry, OSZ). He studied hospitality through an apprenticeship as a chef at the Palace hotel. In between, he travelled and while lying on a beach in Hawaii, he was offered a job in Credit Suisse where he later became a private banker. Tommy took over the hotel in 2014. His family is still involved: His dad, Heinz, who has a great knowledge and experience remains in an advisory capacity while his mother, Elisabeth worked several years in the HR and hospitality area. He has three sisters, Nadine, Sandy and Simone and everyone mucks in when help is needed.

"My philosophy is helping others," he said. "My grandfather bought this hotel from money lent to him partly by the family who owned the Palace hotel. My role as the Managing Director is to encourage and inspire the staff. We are a team and owners can no longer just boss staff around. My right hand is Fabienne at reception who is also my girlfriend."

Ermitage Wellness & Spa Hotel

Dorfstrasse 46
3778 Schönried
Tel. 033 748 0430
welcme@ermitage.ch
www.ermitage.ch

The Ermitage is different from other five-star hotels through its Alpine interiors and laid-back atmosphere which enables people to chill out for days or weeks. It's situated on a sunny terrace above Gstaad in the middle of a park with panoramic view of the surrounding mountains and Saanenland. Ermitage is a world-class hotel with a high quality of service and friendly staff.

A top inducement of the hotel is that it's a veritable oasis of wellness which covers 3,700m² with outdoor and indoor salt water pools (35°C), a heated outdoor sports pool (28°C to 31°C), an aqua dome, 10 saunas and steam baths, massages and varied health treatments.

Another inducement is the ¾ gourmet board which consists of a big buffet breakfast, a lunch with soup and salad, afternoon tea and patisserie and a 5-course dinner menu with choices from gourmet to vegetarian dishes served in eight different dining rooms. The third inducement is the stunning landscape with panoramic views of mountains, hills and loads of fresh air. As Ermitage is located in Schönried, a village outside Gstaad, guests can enjoy the beautiful walk into it or a 10 minute journey by train. The hotel provides a shuttle service to and from the station.

The story of the Ermitage started on November 1, 1977 when Heiner Lutz and Laurenz Schmid bought a small pension. They were pioneers in the field of wellness and today it's one of the largest wellness hotel in Switzerland with 96 rooms. It's open all year round so people can come and benefit from pampering spa treatments including the latest developments such as goats' milk creams.

Romantik Hotel Hornberg

Bahnhofstrasse 36
CH 3777 Saanenmöser
Tel. 033 748 66 88
wilkommen@hotel-hornberg.ch
www.hotel-hornberg.ch

There are family run hotels and family run hotels but the Romantik Hotel Hornberg is one with a difference. It's a place where the family is very visible and participate in events arranged for their guests who are treated like extended family. The 4-star hotel which has 40 rooms including family suites and family rooms is open all year round except for five weeks when they are closed either in April or November for renovations. Children are catered for as there is a playground in the park and sledges are provided in winter. Skiing in and out from the piste as well as a 18-hole golf course nearby. It's a three minute walk from the train station and a food shop is open seven days a week.

Brigitte and Christian Hoefliger von Siebenthal who is the third generation, took over from Brigitte's parents, Elisabeth and Peter von Siebenthal-Wild in 2003. They are imbued with the spirit of Brigitte's grandparents, Werner and Helene von Siebenthal-Hauswirth who opened in the winter of 1936/1937.

"During the winter we advise guests of best skiing of the day, and in summer, we hike with them," said Christian Hoefliger, an affable and dynamic man. "When we organise picnics, I drive up in a military vehicle and cook on an open fire and my wife, for example, can be guiding the hike. It's important to create an emotional connection with guests. A special bonus is when the grandchildren of guests come to stay at the Romantik Hotel Hornberg. One day, I was proud when a male guest returned from a hike and said, 'home at last.'"

Although, Gstaad in the mind of many guests is only open for six months of the year, Christian believes that in the future it will become an all-year round resort. Sustainability and innovation are the main pillars of the destination strategy since guests come here to experience nature and feel good. The resort competes in a very dynamic market worldwide and needs a unique selling point (USP). In addition, there is the socialising because they meet people on the shared activities. There is also a special scheme for the hotel staff called YourGstaad which provides

Romantik Hotel Hornberg.

sports activities, parties, workshops and further education as well as benefits.

"The USP is nature," he said with a smile. "Here we have what most city dwellers don't have: the privilege of sleeping in a calm environment, breathing fresh air, hearing birds in the morning, smelling the rain and the fresh-cut hay, seeing wild flowers growing. There are of course also social motives like meeting up with friends, or going where others go, and that is often also a motivation for people choosing their destination."

The guest's programmes at Romantik Hotel Hornberg is chockfull and caters to all tastes. It varies from cooking classes and boogie woogi events to paper-cutouts with an expert Regina Martin who teaches students to make Christmas cards and visits to cheesemakers in the alpine pastures who still use cauldrons over open fires. A treat is the Tomme Fleurette, a unpasteurised cheese which is best eaten melted or lukewarm. Light and milky on the palate, it has complex flavours that include buttery straw, farmyard, sweet cream and subtle floral notes.

Christian who comes from a village near Zurich, was an apprentice chef and studied at the Business and Hotel Management school, Lucerne where he met Brigitte. He worked among other places in Canada and in Basel for the Grand Circle Travel group.

Chapter 5. Eating

Watch the cows while you eat in a barn or quaff champagne in rustic alpine hut at 1,400m while a top chef cooks meat on a spit or taste unforgettable cuisines in multi-starred restaurants.

Sonnenhof Restaurant.

Sonnenhof Restaurant

Sonnenhofweg 33,
3792 Gstaad
Between Saanen and Schönried
Tel 033744 1023
restaurant.sonnenhof@bluewin.ch
www.restaurantsonnenhof.ch

The Sonnenhof is a story of excellence for over 20 years. The spectacular view of the mountain ranges from the panoramic terrace compliments the inspired French-Italian cuisine. It is well known among le tout-Gstaad. The charming couple, Erich Baumer and his Swedish wife Louise, welcome their guests to the light, elegant, rustic decor of the restaurant.

Erich's cuisine is always of impeccable quality and precision and the two menus include the classics served throughout the year and his weekly proposals. What is most impressive about this Gault Millau starred restaurant (16) is that Erich is a local boy and his natural talent has taken him to the top. But what is most important for him is that he cooks expressly for his client and not to win awards. Louise is known for her highly competent service and enjoys welcoming each guest. She takes care of the ambiance and constantly changes decorations to reflect the seasons and festivities. Above all, she ensures that the guests are comfortable and feel at home.

"When I was young, I wanted to become a pastry chef," said Erich, "but my mother steered me toward becoming a chef as there were more job possibilities. She was right and I started as an apprentice at the Bellevue Hotel under Martin Dalsass who now runs the Michelin- starred Dalsass Talvo restaurant in Champfèr. He sent me to a friend at the German holiday island of Sylt and I experienced a life changing

Erich and Louise Baumer

moment. I was 20 and worked non-stop for three months as we were one staff member short. Such concentrated labour prepared me for the rest of my career."

The signature dishes include the delicate carpaccio of tuna with soy and wasabi and legendary ravioli generously provided with truffles from Périgord. A speciality is pigeon normally served for two. Once it's cooked it's presented to the guest and then taken away to be de-boned.

My companion and I also appreciated the creamed asparagus soup with chervil; the amuse bouche of cod, salmon and quinoa; fillet steak on the stone (with Lamborghini red - Trecote from Umbria), veal shanks (with le Caveau du Cloitre from Aigle) which was cooked for 14 hours and served with mashed potato and green beans and bacon. The desserts too were a treat. Our selections, which were out of this world, was the tonka bean crème brûlée and the delicious light apfelstrudel.

Erich was one of eight siblings and his father was the concierge at the Bellevue hotel for more than 30 years. He was also a ski instructor, worked at the Chesery with Robert Speth and a chef on a private yacht. (See entry, Speth). Erich met Louise who was an aerobics teacher at the English pub in Saanen where he also cooked for one season (1986). They teamed up when he was a chef and manager of the Hirschen in Amriswil near lake Constance. (1991-1999) and have been a formidable team ever since because they compliment each other.

"We heard about the Sonnenhof as a neighbour of mine who ran the restaurant which already had a good reputation wanted to retire," he said. "It was a speciality restaurant serving meat on a hot stone, fondue and raclette. For us, it was a important opportunity as we could return to Gstaad and start our own restaurant. We first rented and later when we bought it, renovated the place and changed the menu - got rid of the cheese smell. Since then we have had success with our two menus. The classics like beef stroganoff, eminence of veal and slow-cooked dishes or the lobster, foie gras (hot or cold) truffle or freshly caught fish. My aim is to satisfy our demanding guests with visually attractive dishes as well as the most appetising food."

Off duty, both Louise and Erich enjoy a game of golf. His special hobby is gardening and he plants flowers of different colours on the tiny hill outside the restaurant. Amonst the flowers, he has several specially carved wooden artworks that include an owl, a marmot, a squirrel and mushrooms. They have two children, Tim who has made his apprenticeship as a cook and Linn who is in administration for hospitality.

Le Grand Chalet

Bagatelle restaurant
Neueretstrasse 43
Tel. 0337487676
info@grandchalet.ch
www.grandchalet.ch

The Grand Chalet is a chalet style hotel on a small hill above the centre of Gstaad with an amazing view of the mountains and valleys. It consists of 23 rooms including two suites and has a small sauna and Turkish bath. The Swiss Alpine decor in the rooms and throughout the hotel is even extended to the fetching dirndls worn by the staff. The hotel also has a gourmet restaurant, La Bagatelle, with an award-winning wine list and over 15,000 bottles. For aficionados of the grape, it's recommended to spend an hour to study the 30 page wine book printed on handmade Himalayan paper.

Pedro Ferreira, the manager and Steve Willié the chef are co-directors of the hotel and restaurant. Pedro has a cosmopolitan background as he was born in Angola, spent several years in Brazil and finally the family settled in Lisbon where his father opened a restaurant. The popular dish was steamed fish head. In 1988, he gained a hospitality diploma in San Sebastian and his first job was at the Park Hotel in Wengen.

"I came to Gstaad in 1997," said Pedro, a charming and elegant man, "and except for two years when I worked for the Hermitage, I have been at the

Steve Willié and Pedro Ferreira

Grand Chalet. I was lucky to work under Franz Rosscogler, the former owner and wine connoisseur who was responsible for the spectacular wine selection. Consequently, any guest will find the right wine for their budget and always at the best quality."

Steve Willié has maintained a high gourmet standard in the restaurant through his continuous appearance in the Gault Millau. He is French and born in Strasbourg. He trained at the catering and hotel management school of Strasbourg before he came to Gstaad to work at the Olden hotel and restaurant. Steve started at the Grand Chalet in 1994 and was named Chef of the Year by the top German business magazine Bilanz in 2011.

"I use fresh, seasonal high quality products and the cuisine can be described as Mediterranean with French regional specialities," said Steve. "The greatest praise for me is the happiness of the guests."

The hotel has selection of gourmet packages with three course, four course (discovery) or five course (gastronomic) lunches or dinners. For the hikers there is not only a pre-packed daily picnic but also a three course gourmet dinner on their return.

The restaurant ambiance is relaxed with attentive service. The food is a delight. It's traditional French and was described by my companion as raffiné which is perfect. Besides the à la Carte, the menu consists of the three course gourmet plat de jour and the market suggestion varies from 'Royal Belgium' caviar to roasted Bresse chicken with Perigord black truffles.

The starters chosen were carpaccio and red tuna tartare and langoustine from South Africa in garlic and parsley butter. With the main, we opted for the saddle of lamb from Sisteron with thyme flowers and titbits of al dente vegetables. It was served with two chops: one rare and the other was well cooked and tastier. Another meat dish included Swiss beaf fillet from the top butcher in Gstaad Robert Bratschi while the fish choice consisted of slices of Brittany sole meunière and poached Alpine salmon. (See entry, Bratschi). There was also a couple of vegetarian dishes like Del Plin ravioli with spinach and ricotta cheese as well as gnocchis with artichokes and chanterelles. For dessert there's the regional meringue and cream but the variation instead is filled with red berries and vanilla cream. A must for chocoholics is the chocolate soufflé Valrhona and absinthe sorbet.

An unusual feature of the Grand Chalet is the zither player, Werner Frei who has been at the hotel for 30 years. The music is beloved by celebrities and guests particularly, children.

Posthotel Rössli

Promenade 10
3780 Gstaad
Tel. 033748 4242
info@posthotelroessli.ch
www.posthotelroessli

Built in 1845, the Posthotel Rössli is the oldest hotel in Gstaad and is situated right in the middle of the pedestrianised village. The building is three-storeys and superior rooms provide good views for events like the fireworks on the Swiss national day on August 1 and the return of the cows from the Alps, Des Alpes festiva , in September.

The hotel is a charming 3-star with 19 rooms including family rooms. Guests can experience authentic Alpine style decor and woodwork as well as the other features of the two centu-y building.

It is run by the fourth generation, Conroy and Nadja Widmer who ensure a warm welcome and respect the tradition of Swiss quality hospitality. The two restaurants serve traditional food including the signature dishes of calves liver and rösti and as well as smoked tongue and fondue.

Conroy who grew up in Gstaad, never had any doubts that he was going to follow in the family tradition. As a teenager, he was proud that he could make a vegetable soup and polenta cheese. Later, he servec his apprenticeship at local hotels such as the Palace and the Park. In the mid-1990s, he had the opportunity of travelling to the US where he visited ski areas teaching ski-jumping and working in local restaurants.

"I was impressed by the diversity of the food and creativity of the menus in America," he said. "When I returned, I studied at the School of Hospitality in Thun. It was important as later when I took over the restaurant/hotel, I could implement the knowledge. One of the first things I did was to integrate the two menus of the stubli and the restaurant."

The emphasis is on fresh local products and Conroy works closely with farmers who supply quality products for seasonal dishes such as game or lamb for spring. He is also active on the wastage front. At one time each guest received a fruit basket and anything that was not eaten was thrown away. So to stop waste, the basket was discarded.

"It's important for guests to enjoy their stay," said Nadja, "It doesn't have to perfect but special in a good way. When I first arrived from Germany to work in Gstaad, my first impression was that people were living in a postcard. The view from Schönried to the valley below was wonderful. I saw the MOB train winding its way through the Saanen valley and it reminded me of one of the toy trains."

Brasserie/ Wintergarden

Sporthotel Victoria
Promenade 72
Tel. 033 7484422
info@victoria-gstaad.ch
www.victoria-gstaad

The restaurant is known for its solid comfort food which is well priced and includes old-fashioned Swiss specialities such as sliced veal and head of veal. There is also a selection of pastas like spaghetti with olive oil, garlic and chillies.

The recommended starter is a salad with mixed greens, bacon bits and egg served with the Special Victoria dressing which is popular with guests. Many ask for the recipe which is a secret but are placated with a serving to take home.

The sliced veal (Zürcher Kalbsgeschnetzeltes) consists of thin slices, cooked quickly and served with mushrooms, onions in a demiglace brown sauce. The accompaniment is sautéed rösti. The head of veal consists of the soft meat from the cheeks and nose served with vinaigrette sauce, boiled potatoes and green salad. Another meat dish is tripe in tomato sauce served with boiled potatoes and salad. For British tastes, there is cold roast beef with French fries and tartare sauce.

Besides the pasta, there are 15 sorts of pizzas on the menu and even a cheese burger served with French fries. For those who like fish, perch is served.

Desserts include the unique apple tart with egg white, apple and hazel nuts which is served with vanilla ice cream and the crema Catalana, a Portuguese variation of crème brûlée which has cinnamon and lemon peel rather than vanilla as ingredients.

Restaurant La Sarine

Hotel Arc-en-ciel
Egglistrasse 24
Tel. 033 7484343
info@arc-en-ciel.ch
www.arc-en-ciel.ch

The restaurant is in a wonderful setting with its mountain views and the terrace/wintergarden which can seat 300 is the most popular area. The ambiance indoors with the contemporary rustic decor is relaxed. The menus are diverse with a wide choice of salads, starters, soups, meat, fish, pasta, vegetarian (even a Vegan dish consisting of pumpkin ragout with sautéed boletus, nuts and pear) and desserts galore. My companion and I found two dishes outstanding. The salad Arc-en-ciel with trimmings of bacon and croutons and the fresh trout which was alive immediately before cooked au Blau or grilled.

The restaurant was known for its pizzas right from the start and the pizzeria with its wood-fired oven is in the oldest part of the restaurant. A Neapolitan was the first pizziolo and his special recipe is still used. Besides pizzas with the crispy dough, you can enjoy antipasti and pasta. You can also pre-order and collect.

The restaurant prides itself on seasonal and regional specialities. The fresh local products are much in evidence such as the meat from the Buuregemetzg Gstaad, fruit and vegetables from Schmid in Saanen, bread from Chnusper-becke bakery in Gstaad, dairy products from the Molkerei Gstaad and ice cream from Ruci Gstaad.

Appetising dishes include grilled garlic bread with pine nuts and Zucchini tapenade or Saanenland goat's cheese with caramelised figs; penne Manzo with marinated beef, red onions and pepperoni; Viennese veal escalope; plum sorbet with plum brandy; crepes with nutella and sour cream ice cream.

Lac Retaud

Restaurant/Hotel
Route du Lac Retaud 4
1865 Les Diablerets
Tel. 0244921368
contact@lacretaud.ch
www.lacretaud.ch

Franz Wehren is a leading restauranteur who owns the award winning L'Auberge in Hermance, Geneva and the Lac Retaud opposite Glacier 3000 in the Col du Pillon, which he runs with Fabrizio Adamo. He is an enigmatic man, who has the presence of a television show host and for the past 35 years has staged exceptional events

Lac Retaud.

in the Gstaad region.

When it comes to giving a good party he is a past master. He is a man about town and a board member of the Gstaad Yacht Club.

"At my hotel in Saanenmõser, I organised fantastic events for the A-listers," said Franz. "The period between 1985-1990 was great because people wanted to have genuine fun. We would go heli-skiing and have apré-ski parties. On one occasion, we filled a bath with spaghetti and had a contest to see who could eat the most. The winner was given a balloon ride at 4am. On another, I organised together with the playboy Gunter Sachs a Miss Winter contest and the winner was on the front page of the German magazine, Blick. Nowadays, by comparison, the A-listers are much more low-key and restrained about fun."

Franz Wehren comes from a prominent local family. His great grandfather, Ruedi Wehren, was a teacher and founded the Anzeiger von Saanen in 1880. (See entry, Müller Median). However, Franz has hospitality in his DNA as his grandfather, Rudolf was the hotel pioneer. After the advent of the Montreux Oberland Bernois (MOB) railway in 1905, Rudolf was the first to see an opportunity for tourism and opened several hotels.

Franz grew up Saanenmõser and from an early age helped his parents in the hotel. He was interested in becoming a chef de cuisine and was first apprenticed at the famous Park hotel in Villars. Later, he cooked at the Grappe d'Or in Lausanne and then went on to gain more experience in Michelin-starred restaurants in Manhattan, New York where, on his days off, he cooked privately for Rita Hayworth and her daughter, the Princess Yasmina Ali Khan. Lac Retaud is in a spectacular setting with the emerald green lake below and the snow covered peaks above. It's different from mountain restaurants where the traditional fare is limited to fondue and rösti. Here the fondue is served with black truffles and the beef tartare with truffles sauce. The signature dishes are light, chic and contemporary. The is ultimate compliment is that it is often patronised by a restaurateur from Gault & Millau with 17 ratings. The restaurant also has a private room for special occasions and it is not unusual to find people like Roman Polanski celebrating his birthday there.

The starters vary from a trio of fish that includes trout, fera rilettes and marinated fera some of which are caught in the lake below to the sucker arm of octopus on red cabbage surrounded by cubes of sweet potato. The mains are diverse from boiled beef in a vegetable broth and fish lasagne to stuffed duck with onion paste and foie gras.

During the game season, besides the standard Swiss dish with Brussel sprouts, red cabbage, chestnuts and spätzli there is choice of venison served with polenta taragna or tartare of venison with crispy polenta taragna. Desserts are tempting such as meringue with gruyere double cream or the unique creamy, thick chestnut ice cream. Two vintages that are outstanding from the wine list include the Grand Cru Clos du Crosex Grillé which is a Syrah and the Grand Cru St Saphorin chateau de Glérolles.

16 Art Bar Restaurant

Mittelgaessli 16
3792 Saanen
Tel. 033 748 1616
contact@16eme.ch
www.16eme.ch

Butcher, Thai & Burger Take-Away and Wine

Dorfstrasse 70
3792 Saanen
Tel. 033 748 1616
contact@16eme.ch
www.16eme.ch

The 16 Art - Bar - Restaurant is located in the historic Saanen in the picturesque Mittelgässli 16.

Gastronomy and art merge in the former bell foundry from the 18th Century. Grill specialties and an innovative, regional cuisine with fine wines. Simon and his brother Nik Buchs run the restaurant.

"We are born further down the train track near Lenk," said Simon, the younger brother. "I trained as an interior decorator while Nik became a cook. We first thought of doing catering 'out of the box' without a place. Our first job was working for an event company called Experience." (See entry, Experience).

When the butcher shop closed in Saanen, the Buchs opened their shop which is a Thai & Burger takeaway.

Hotel Olden

Promenade 35
Tel. 0337484950
info@hotelolden.com
www.hotelolden.com

The Hotel Olden and restaurant is a perfect fit for Gstaad as it's popular with A-listers who have chalets, the locals and visitors. Gstaad's smallest hotel has one of the finest cellars with some 14,000 bottles. It contains around 350 different wines including gems such as Petrus and Château Lafite Rothschild wines. Some of the most expensive vintages are valued at over CHF 32,000.

The Olden is a luxurious cosy refuge with 12 rooms and a family atmosphere. It's an institution which is filled with memories of past celebrities such as Liz Taylor and Richard Burton who played Yahtzee. (See entry, Hans-Ueli Tschanz.)

"We know all the guests by name and for many of them it's like coming home to their living room," said Ermes Elsener, the director. "We're fully booked at Christmas as most of our guests from all over the world tend to stay for at least 10 days."

The Olden has unique dishes that you can boast about to friends back home like the foot-long Milanese veal with rocket salad and cherry tomatoes and the Tower salad called Oriental and served with sautéed prawns. Spaghettini Sciué Sciué (translated as quick, quick) is a firm favourite and the grilled assortment of fish (whole sea bass) and meat (lamb cutlets).

Besides the tiramisu and hazelnut parfait glazed with raspberries and pistachio sauce, the top dessert is Moelleux au chocolat with caramel slightly salted ice cream and crunchy almonds.

Swiss traditional wrestling aka Schwingen.

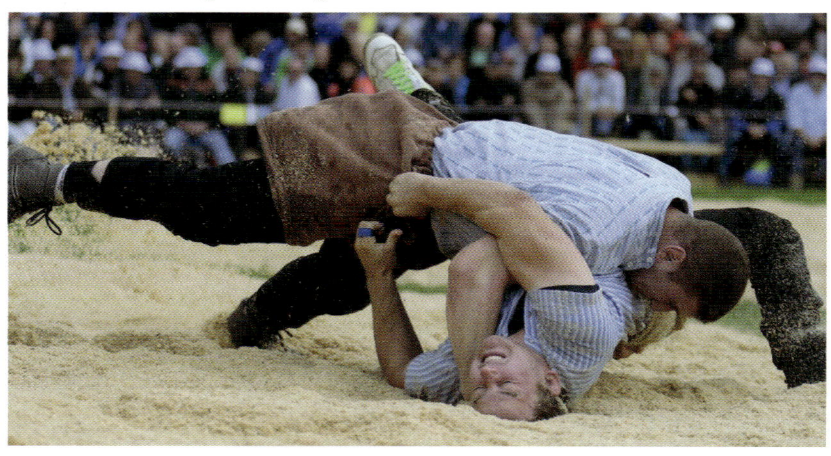

Chapter 6. Banks & Business

How to get more bang for your bucks, whether buying a property or car, sponsorship, experiences, archiving or publishing.

UBS Switzerland AG

Promenade 66
P.O.Box 286
Tel. 033 748 8511
www.ubs.com/standorte/schweiz/gstaad/promenade-66

The UBS bank in Gstaad is considered to be the local boutique of an international bank. Situated in the tourist hotspot, it has access to everything and is a global window.

"A substantial part of our clients are foreign and a typical one is someone who falls in love with the region and ends up by buying a property," said Thomas Bohnenblust, Executive Director. "The first thing he needs is a bank account. Next a bank with facilities of international wealth management and wealth planning."

Thomas has been with UBS as man and boy for 33 years. He was born in Thun, grew up in Spiez and joined the bank as an apprentice in 1985. He gradually worked his way up in the bank. His first job was at the cash desk in retail at Geneva airport. In 1997, he changed to wealth management.

"I liked the advisory role with clients and was promoted to wealth management and branch leadership in 2000," he said. "I found it was important to engender trust and confidence over the longterm. It's also important to establish an emotional link with your client and give them a special experience. I once went on a four-man bobsled with a client and it was an exhilarating ride at a speed of 135km per hour. It was a moment of a lifetime. On another occasion, we presented a special event of Schwingen or Swiss wrestling for our clients. This again created a high level of emotions to show an old Swiss tradition to our guests."

"My philosophy is always to give my best to a task or a job," he continued, "and then later you will get recognition. It's always better to remain yourself."

Manuel Blanco,

Credit Suisse

Promenade 67
P.O. Box 315
Tel. 033 748 9797
www.credit-suisse.com

Manuel Blanco, Managing Director at Credit Suisse, is a good example of the new breed of Swiss Bankers. He not only follows closely the markets but with his team he also takes the necessary measures. As Head of Market Area Gstaad, he views the branch as a showroom for all its investment divisions worldwide. He has dual Master Degrees of Science in Wealth Management at Rochester (NY) University (2016-2018) as well of Advanced Studies in Finance at Bern University.

"Our goal here is to give our clients a life without financial concerns," he said. "It's our flagship branch, an inspiring place like the iconic glass cube Apple Store on 5th Avenue, New York. The bank carefully listens to the needs of clients, whether it's related to the family, business, wealth or society, and takes the right measures that are defined together with the client. Credit Suisse aims to be a leading wealth manager with strong investment banking capabilities and positions itself as a bank for Switzerland, a bank for entrepreneurs, a bank for the next generation and a bank for the digital world. Our relationship managers take them by the hand and connect them with the right place and the right experts within Credit Suisse."

Blanco who has a dual Spanish/Swiss nationality was born in Bern where he was educated. His mother was Swiss and his father came from Malaga. He is banker through and through having started as an apprentice at Credit Suisse. He has chalked up some 27 years, most of it with Credit Suisse except for a decade with another Swiss bank where he gained international experience. He is a pan-European, multilingual and speaks English, German, French, Spanish and Italian.

"I'm proud of the Swiss Banking Industry which went through huge changes and still is amongst the best in the world," he said. "In particular, Credit Suisse which was founded in 1856 by Alfred Escher who was a pioneer and engendered the bank with a strong entrepreneurial spirit. Two of the projects he supported were the Swiss railways and the Gotthard tunnel. What we provide today for a client is knowhow and comprehensive advice which results in generating added value for them. Instead of having different opinions on markets in different parts of the bank, we bring together everything in one place, the "Credit Suisse House View." It's a holistic experience for clients."

Football is his passion and he played as a junior for the Young Boys Bern. He believes that success is based on diversity and a team in banking should include different people with different skills from different backgrounds. It's analogous to top teams in the Premier league in football.

Jürg von Allmen

Saanen Bank

Bahnhofstrasse 2
3792 Saanen
Tel. 033 748 4646
info@saanenbank.ch
www.saanenbank.ch

Saanen Bank is the regional bank with its headquarters in Saanen and branches in Gstaad, Gsteig, Lauenen and Schönried. It was founded in 1874 and is proud of its heritage of having began as a savings and loan institution for local farmers and tradesmen. Today, the bank handles funds of CHF 1.3 billion and offers corporate, private and retail banking.

The CEO is Jürg von Allmen who not only has national banking experience with Credit Suisse but has been with the regional bank for some 15 years. The Board of Directors comprises Victor Steimle, President (Business Economist), Vice President Daniel Matti (CEO Chaletbau Matti), Marianne Kropf (pharmacist), Regula van der Velde (auditor), Michael Teuscher (governor), Peter Weissen (engineer) and Erich von Siebenthal, (farmer and parliamentarian).

"The bank has a balancing act with one foot in the important agriculture sector and the other in international private banking," he said. "About 20% to 30% of our clients are international and they appreciate our regional roots. Just as visitors in the area like to buy local products like Simmentaler meat from the butcher or mountain cheese in the dairy, they want to work with a regional bank. On the other side, we are enthusiastic sponsors of local events whether they be agricultural shows, yodelling or sports like tennis and cultural highlights such as the Menuhin Festival. We're not interested in national media coverage but rather the praise and compliments from the locals."

Von Allmen comes from Spiez where his father was a school teacher. He followed in his father's footsteps and studied education from 1983-1988 at the teacher's seminar at Spiez.

Since then he gained diplomas in financial expertise and management at University of Applied Sciences Northwestern Switzerland and St. Gallen university among others. Before he joined Saanen Bank 2003, he held various positions at Swiss Volksbank and Credit Suisse. In 2008, he was appointed CEO.

"Among the various services we offer is a special one for young people," he said. "It ranges from birth to 25. A unique account is "Free 25" which has the advantages such as preferential interest rate and free credit cards. In fact, students from the two schools Le Rosey and J.F.Kennedy play an important role as they are the driving force of the international residents in our community. Parents take their first or second home in the region while they study here and there's a trend for former students return to us and buy holiday homes."

Mũller Medien AG

Kirchstrasse 6
Tel. 033 748 8874
info@mmedien.ch
www.mmedien.ch

Frank Mũller is Gstaad's local newspaper and magazine publisher. He produces the Anzeiger von Saanen, Gstaad My Love and GstaadLife. The aims of the newspaper are the same as when the local teacher, Ruedi Wehren, founded it in 1880: to offer a platform to villagers. They could air their views or grievances in the pages of the Anzeiger and in so doing bring harmony in Saanenland. Today, the newspaper, which is bi-weekly, has a circulation of around 5,000 copies. The company also publishes books, calendars, posters, and cards.

"I'm proud that we continue the same tradition in the newspaper today," said Frank, the dynamic third generation who owns the company together with his brother Richard. "We don't polarise our readers, we're not into sensationalism. We carefully read through reader's letters. If some are biased, we act as a mediator and publish both sides of the issue. Of course, the concerns have changed

Frank M�ller

radically since the 19th century. Today it's about the investment in cable cars, the rigid building restrictions and healthcare facilities - the local hospital closure caused a furore."

He is innovative and when digital publishing was introduced, he helped develop a system, which can be used by small publishers and is economical. It's called LocalPoint and has been taken up by several other publishers in Switzerland. He was also involved in the launch of a new newspaper, the Frutigländer, which covers another part of the Berner Oberland.

Frank grew up in Gstaad and during the holidays worked at the Anzeiger inserting stories. Later, after gaining his matura in Bern, he studied engineering before taking over the publishing company from his father in 1989. He enjoys ski touring and playing ice hockey.

Kultur Engagement

Walischistrasse 29
Saanen
Tel. 033744 7456
Info@kultur-engagment.ch
www.kultur-engagement.ch

Kultur Engagement is a company which organises sponsors for cultural events, film financing, project investments, publications and fundraising for art exhibitions all over the world. Since 1999, Gstaad Menuhin Festival & Academy has been its major client.

The company is run by a husband and wife team, Hans-Ueli Tschanz and Marlène Tschanz. Hans-Ueli who is a fundraiser par excellence and won the International Sponsoring Award in Hamburg for the best concept for the Swiss film, *Mein Name ist Eugen*. He is an expert in tourism, a doyen on Gstaad and has extensive experience in dealing with celebrities and VVIPs. He is also the chief editor of the prestigious annual magazine, *Gstaad My Love*.

"I've seen Gstaad in its changeover period when I was Tourist Director," he said. "I remember the period when Hedi Donizetti, owner of the Olden hotel for 40 years held sway over the aperitif at 5pm when she swilled and drank her dry sherry. She was surrounded by celebrities like David Niven who danced the twist there until 4am, Curt Jürgens who once asked 'Am I stupid or why do I always pay for everyone? As well as Ava Gardner, Sophia Loren, Jackie Kennedy,

Hans-Ueli Tschanz

Julie Andrews, Roman Polanski, Jack Nicholson, Roger Moore and Gunter Sachs who was a regular."

"They mixed with locals who sat at tables playing cards," he continued, "and the paparazzi clicking away particularly when Liz Taylor entered. She had great charisma. Then Bernie Ecclestone took over from Hedi and it marked another period when film and showbiz gave way to top financial investors." (See entry, Olden hotel).

Hans-Ueli was born in Bern where he was educated. His mother was a teacher while father was a military officer who trained national service recruits. He studied for a commercial diploma and his first job was with Kuoni where he was a ground operator in London. Later, he worked in guest services for tourists at Zurich airport and as tourist director in Brunnen on the lake Lucerne. His final position in tourism was in Gstaad (1986-1992) where he was Tourist Director. He joined the Menuhin Festival as director in 1992 until 1999 when he left to start Kultur Engagement but he is still on the board of the festival.

"I took over the festival while Yehudi Menuhin was still alive and together with his assistant Eleanor Hope we ran it," he said. "In 1997, Gidon Kremer was appointed as Yehudi's successor and his modernistic style was unsuited to the audiences. (See entry, Christoph Müller). This led to a decrease in revenue and attendees. I left after two years and the festival became Kultur Engagement's client. Another event, was a film and music festival, Cinemusic, which I organised with Julie Andrews and Blake Edwards. It was the second cultural footprint in Gstaad and featured showbiz stars such as Liza Minelli, Quincy Jones, Michel Legrand, Henry Mancini and Claude Nobs from Montreux Jazz Festival. It ended in 1998 but is worth reviving."

Hans-Ueli was instrumental in changing the editorial content of the magazine, Gstaad My Love to reflect that his interviews portray people who are meaningful for the region and the outside world. He was also involved in the publication of 100 years of the

Palace and was a researcher for the major work by Dr Rolf Steiger on Gstaad and the Menuhins.

"What people don't understand about Gstaad is that compared to Davos or St. Moritz, it's a small place," he said. "The philosophy is not to expand but to remain at the size it's now which is optimal. Also it's a discrete destination with a lot of chalets and not a place for mega partying, superstar cars or ostentation."

And the future of Gstaad? There is a project that Hans-Ueli favours, Les Arts Gstaad, which is to be a replacement for the festival tent. It's a concert hall which is designed by the architect Rudy Ricciotti and will be built in the centre of village next to the station.

Ledi Garage Feutersoey Ag

Gewerbestrasse 18
3784 Feutersoey
Tel. 033 7558585
ledi-garage@gstaad.ch
www.ledigarage.ch

Ledi garage is a Land Rover and Range Rover dealership which repairs all makes of cars and offers a collection service. It's unique with its aluminium body shop which enables the garage also to repair new models like Ferrari, Tesla, Lamborghini or Jaguar which have aluminium structures. In addition, it has experience in rallies and repairing vintage cars.

Hansueli Brand runs the leading family owned garage which installed the first certified aluminium body shop in Europe in 2016. He is nicknamed 'Mr Range Rover' and is also a racing driver who won the Tour Auto France and a man with two identities. He raced against Stirling Moss several times in the Tour Auto Optik France and was the first Swiss winner in 2005 in an Aston Martin. He also participated with clients in the races to Dakar, Beijing and founded the Gstaad Automobile Club with Isabelle de Stadler and Stéphane Gutzwiller. He runs Ledi Garage with his two sons, Fabian who is a certificated body and paint shop technician and Dominik who is in charge of administration and after sales service for all the customers. For the second year running, he was awarded no 1 for Land Rover Customer satisfaction in Switzerland.

"Land Rover is my life;" he said. "It's a brand which has the most emotion. As a young man I had dreamt of becoming a carpenter but as the occupation was over subscribed, I became a car mechanic instead. And I've never looked back. My father died young and left five children (three boys and two girls) who were farmed out to families. I was educated as a farm boy and learnt a lot about life, animals and hard work. In 1976, I became an apprentice with the local garage Gehret which had Land Rover cars and later went to Geneva to work with a dealership."

Hansueli returned to Feutersoey with

Hansueli, Dominik and Fabian Brand

a partner Bernhard Lammers in 1981 and founded Ledi Garage with Ford, Saab and Land Rover dealerships. In 2001, they celebrated 20 years with winning the Best dealer award. After 35 years, his partner left and he established a new company with his sons in 2015. Today, they have 13 staff plus two apprentices.

"I am proud that I have customers in Switzerland and all over Europe," he said. "At first nobody could spell Feutersoey so I would repeat it to them several times. Later, the name became a joke between us and whenever, they found a car from us they would send a photo of the number plate with Feutersoey on it. I learnt to speak other languages from famous customers and I discovered how important communication is. My advice to young people is don't press a button on your smart phone that takes you into a virtual world. Do it in the real world."

Hansueli has led a remarkable life. His journey took him from cutting the grass of chalets in Oberbort as a boy to later selling cars to the owners of chalets who became his friends. His two identities arose from the fact he is named Hansueli Brand on his car license and later he found that his father had put Johane Ulrich on his birth certificate. He is most proud of his two sons. His wife Beate is a trained podiatrist and has a beauty salon in Gstaad which makes her happy.

"She is very important for our business," said Hansueli, "because she is the heart and spirit of our family, our passion and helps us to be professional and maintain high quality."

Raphael Faux

Chalet Le Pont
1659 Rougemont
Tel. 079 673 6005
info@gstaadphotography.com

The man behind the lens that captures all aspects of the social scene in Gstaad is Raphael Faux. The resort is fortunate to have such a professional photographer. One has only to pick up a copies of local publications and you will see his creative portraits and photos. He works for private and corporate clients as well as covering important events including the Menuhin Festival.

"I prefer to shoot when subjects are unaware as they tend to be more natural," he said. "With landscapes everything here in the region is picture postcardy so I try to get behind the cliche."

Raphael was born in Lorraine, France and trained at the Magnum agency in Paris where he met photographers such as Robert Capa. The agency gave photographers the freedom to record what they saw without having to work for the agendas of newspapers and

Raphael Faux

magazines. He lived in Paris and was once invited to come in Gstaad by a friend. He stayed for three months and in 2007 moved there permanently.

"When I left Magnum in 1998 my head was full of photos from journalists in war zones," he said, "I was inspired and went to Indonesia and suddenly found myself in the middle of a revolution. President Suharto was toppled and there was violence and chaos in the streets. When I returned, I had an exhibition of my photos. But life has moved on and today everyone has a Leica in their pocket. I use an Alpa camera which is the most sophisticated camera available for architecture and landscape."

Rolf T. Schneider

Rialtostrasse 15
Tel. 033 7488811
rts.law@gstaad.ch
www.gstaad-notariat.ch

Rolf T. Schneider is a lawyer for all seasons and situations. He is both a notary and an advocate with 40 years experience. He was born in Biel, studied at Bern university, came to Gstaad for his internship and never left. Today, he is a pillar of the establishment and a trusted source when the situation calls for competent consultation or effective lobbying. He has taken on numerous jobs over the years for the local authorities, tourism and the industry sectors. He knows Gstaad's chalet and hotel clients like nobody else and loves Saanenland as a "Kraftort" i.e. a place to rejuvenate oneself.

"My job is to make the life easier for the client even if I have to deal with several heirs," he said. "Sometimes the solution is difficult and requires diplomacy, a bit of psychology and even mediation. As a notary I protect the interest of both parties. But above all, I find that every case is different and I'm proud that 99% of my clients are happy and become friends. I go the extra mile and advise them on schools for their children, give the name of a good dentist, etc."

The services offered vary from real estate transactions of all kinds such as purchase permits for foreigners, company incorporation and restructuring of wills, marriage and inheritance contracts as well as tax and inheritance inventories. Rolf can also arrange financial matters like mortgages and bank loans.

"I think today in the era of rapid progress," he said, "you have to work hard and play hard even more for a balance. When I mention work, I mean do something you like not just for success. I'm lucky as I live in Gstaad which is a little paradise. It has nature, water, fresh air, the four seasons, 350 working farmers and 8,000 cows."

Béatrice Stahel

MC AVOCATS Sàrl/
MC ATTORNEYS LLC

Promenade 76
Tel. 0333358090
bstahel@mcattorneysllc@.com
www.mcattorneysllc.com

MC ATTORNEYS LLC is a boutique law firm with both Swiss (Geneva/Sion/Crans-Montana) and international connections. It was co-founded by two business lawyers, Gilles Crettol and Béatrice Stahel. Advice is provided on a wide range of legal matters including banking and real estate law under the various categories such as brokerage, investment legislation, etc.

"Our typical client is international or English/French speaking and domiciled in Monaco," said Béatrice who is a binational - Swiss/British. "In the main, they are institutional clients who are already active and operational or wish to implement or develop their presence locally. There are also wealthy individuals who wish to take up residence in Switzerland."

Some of the complex cases can involve a foreign client who has a second residence in Gstaad but is domiciled in Monaco with real estate in Geneva and having an international inheritance. However, their experience extends to dealing with company-related legal issues and monitoring domestic and international litigations and arbitrations.

Béatrice studied law at Geneva university and was admitted to the Swiss bar in 2007. Her first position was at De Pfyffer & Associés from 2005-2010 before she joined Monfrini Crettol & Partners and was appointed the Manager of the Sion branch, Valais.

Experience SA

Waldmattenstrasse 5
3778 Schönried b.Gstaad
Tel. 0337488666
info@experience.ch
www.experience.ch

Gstaad is a demanding place and Experience has a way of satisfying events that people want to celebrate and have as a souvenir for the rest of their lives. Unique locations for memorable events include three Alpine huts and a space at the top of a glacier. Experience also offers a customised event which you can design yourself and team activities.

The highlight of any visit to a mountain resort is to experience something totally extraordinary for example spending a night in a rustic hut built in 1786 and being welcomed with an intimate dinner cooked on an open fire. Other options include a cream tea with meringues and cheese and being serenaded by alphorns or dancing to a folk trio; enjoying a fondue in a genuine alpine hut and later going for a coach ride along the mountain paths; and a 20 minute flight in a helicopter which will take you to an alpine hut with stunning views of the Valais including the Matterhorn while you quaff champagne, relish roasted potatoes with the famous local tomme cream cheese and finish with homemade tart made in a old-fashioned wood oven.

Experience has a good reputation for organising events and when one meets Adrian Stocker, it's easy to realise why. He's a smiler and keeps his cool under pressure. "I never try to say no because it's not in my nature but I like to find solutions," he said with a grin, "For example, I'd just organised a truck with equipment to prepare the barn for an event when I received a call for tents at an another event because it was raining. As I have a stock of tents, they were dispatched immediately."

Adrian was born in Simmental where his father is a dairy farmer with 80 cows. He grew up on the farm and learnt to ski in Gstaad where his younger sister taught at the ski school. During his national service he became an officer of the infantry. His leadership skills were honed on persuasion and showing an example.

"Clients who come to us can expect an authentic emotional experience and not a showoff, a Schickimicki," he said. "Of course you can go to a mountain lake and grill sausages but we like to make it perfect. Arrive at the alpine hut before sunrise or sunset. Arrange that you sleep under the stars and create a romantic moment. The real luxury is to spend a simple moment with the right people in an authentic setting that makes an indelible and heartfelt occasion."

The events vary from weddings, seminars, outdoor activities to cocktails and dinners. Some locations are available for most of the year while others are limited from November to April, May to October or mid-June to August. Alpine huts like Les Ouges (1,300m) which is above Rougement and 30 minutes by car can cater for 30 to 170 guests.

"I'm very calm which helps in the case of tense moments," he said. "A lot comes together in a short time and one can't plan or improvise 100%. When working in nature you can't negotiate and it imposes conditions on you. My reward is to see the expressions of surprise or amazement on the faces of people who come to the event."

Gstaad Airport

Oeystrasse 29
3792 Saanen
Tel. 033 748 8422
marc.steiner@gstaad-airport.ch
www.gstaad-airport.ch

Gstaad airport (LSGK) is a non-towered airport without an air traffic control unit. It's located in the Bern Oberland at an altitude of 1,008m (3,307ft). Schengen flights need to advise the airport three hours in advance of their arrival while non-Schengen require notification until 15.30 of the previous day. The aircraft will then be met by customs and police officers on arrival.

The two airlines, Air Glaciers and Air Sarina which serve the airport are not based there. Air Glaciers operates helicopters and provides visitors with a taxi service, sightseeing and heli-sking on snow-covered peaks with great descents. Experienced flying instructors are available for training flights. Air Sarina is an aircraft management company that offers services for private aircraft owners. They include maintenance, administrative jobs, flight preparations, running international flights and booking charters as well as the recruitment of aircrew. Flying instructors are available for training such as taking off and landing on short Alpine runways such as glaciers.

Gstaad airport has a runway of 1,400 m (4,593 ft) and the length limits the type of aircraft which can take-off or

Gstaad airport.

land. This includes a variety of small aircraft from a Piper PA-31, Antonov An-72, De Havilland Canada DHC - 6, ATR 42, Bombadier Dash 8 Q300 to Pilatus PC-12, Embraer Legacy, Cessna Citation, SAAB 340, a Gulfstream G650 and Bombadier Regional Jet CRJ-200.

"The airport is open during the day and 50% of aircraft landing at the airport are turboprops," said Marc Steiner, the manager and former Swissair and Lufthansa pilot who flew Boeing 747s. "The helicopters comprise some 30% of the traffic. The airport is under private ownership and is headed by Walter Egger who is president." (See entry, Walter Egger).

The Board of directors include Marcel Bach, Walter Egger, Andrea Scherz, Beat Marti and Marc Steiner.

Mount10 AG

Haldenstrasse 5
Switzerland
Tel. 041 726 0320
Support 041 726 0328
info@mount10.ch
www.mount10.ch

There is a unique facility in Gstaad. It's a Swiss Fort Knox in the mountain next to the airport and is resistant to any civilian or military threat. But the valuables it guards is not gold but data which is under 24-hour monitoring by a double-guided OperationCenter.

"We selected Gstaad because of its accessibility," said Christoph Oschwald who runs the facility, Mount 10, with his partner Hans Pieter Baumann. "Clients can fly in and out and if they need to stay overnight we have two luxury apartments at their disposal. There's also more than one valley and five roads in. There's no risk of flooding and the fortress is earthquake-proofed."

Currently, they have 40,000 servers and 3,500 clients of which 20% are international.

Bibliothek Saanenland Library

Kirchgemeindehaus Gstaad
Tel. 033 744 5330
info@bibliotheksaanenland.ch

There are librarians and librarians but Silvia Bircher is special as she is an Anglophile. She runs the small library in Gstaad which opened in 1977 and has some 11,000 books. Mainly German books for women readers and for children. She also has an English section with a mixed selection of thrillers, novels and non-fiction which visitors and tourists would find interesting.

Silvia Bircher

"I started reading Enid Blyton books such as the Famous Five and by 12, I'd graduated to adult literature like Angelique," said Silvia who is a charming woman. "It was quite an adventure for me as I learnt about the 17th century France and America. What was exciting was that it was a series and I could look forward to reading some 12 books."

Silvia was born in the canton of Solothurn and at the age of 30 gained her diploma in librarian administration. She married and has a son. Her other job is administrator of the Reformed church Saanenland-Gsteig.

Chapter 7. Real Estate

Locals that deliver Gold standard chalets, renovate farmhouses with several storeys below with swimming pools, gyms and car collections, demolish buildings and sell your houses worldwide.

Addor AG

Civil engineering and transport

Gsteigstrasse 156
Tel. 033 744 24 72
info@addor-ag.ch
www.addor-ag.ch

Addor AG which is a family owned and operated business, was founded in 1954 in Lauenen by Simon Addor. The company has completed quality and cost effective projects for over 65 years. The services vary from transport to Europe, demolition, excavation, road construction, heavy lifting, containers, landfill management to tipper and dumping transport, snow removal and gravel processing.

They are always looking for innovation and new equipment to do their job. Their range includes the state-of-art quick change "Oil-Quick" that makes it possible to change the excavator attachments within a few seconds without manual assistance; and tipper transports for gravel, stone, concrete, excavation or other materials, whether sideways or backwards tilted with semi-trailer or five-axle dump truck. A recent addition is an excavator for demolition with a high reach of 19.5m and weighs over 40 tons. Another aspect is their ecological policy for non-polluting machines and recycling of wood and concrete.

"Our aim is to have the most modern equipment to carry out work as efficiently and quickly as possible," said Heinz Addor, the second generation to run the company. "We take great pride in every project completed from beginning to end. Our company was one of the first in Switzerland to have a gps system which can map out the land in 3-D prior to excavation."

It's every boy's dream to play with toy diggers and loaders but few have the

From L to R: Marco Addor, Daniela Addor, Anja Meier, Patrick Addor, Heinz Addor and wife Ruth

chance to do it when they grow up. Heinz Addor is one of the lucky ones because he became an apprentice with his father after school at the age 16. He began on the loader and digger and gained his license to drive trucks. It was an exciting period from 1974-1982. Later, he moved to the administration department as a construction supervisor. He learnt over time that it was a hard job as his father worked 130%.

"In 1982, I was appointed Manager," he said, "and we employed ten people. Our fleet consisted of five trucks and we had eight construction machines. I took over the company in 1993 and several years later, we moved the head office to Grund in Gstaad. In 2010, we acquired Gehret AG with 13 employees, five trucks and 13 construction machines."

Today they have grown to 65 staff, 27 trucks and several construction machines. One of the first things he did was to expand their transport operations to compensate for the seasonal fluctuations. They extended their routes to Spain and the UK.

"What I'm most proud of is that the company is family run," said Heinz. "My wife Ruth manages the administration and accounting and the third generation have joined - my son Patrick, daughter Daniela and her husband Marco. As most of our work is carried out locally, we support local events and invest in its future."

Mösching Forst

Schibeweg 18
Tel. 079 294 6970
moesching.be@hotmail.com

Martin Mösching is the umpteenth generation of his family who creates wooden roof shingles. Fine examples of the traditional art can be seen on the roofs of the Saanen church and the Gstaad chapel. An axe splits wood from a short log to make lengths similar to tiles which are laid on each other to cover the roof.

"The shingles are durable and can last some 40 years or 60-70 years if impregnated," said Martin Mösching whose family owns forests and a farm. "The trees must be carefully selected and be in a dry area in the shade of the forest. Otherwise if it's in the sun, the wood splits easily. I served no apprenticeship as my father took me into the forest and explained things to me. I did the same to my sons."

Today, the trend is to have shingles inside the house for a ceiling. The family team consists of Mathias, his brother Benjamin and his wife Karin and their father Martin Mösching.

Jaggi Architecture and Interior Design

Suterstrasse 1
Tel. 033744 2688
info@jaggi.swiss
www.jaggi.swiss

The firm's style of architecture is a combination of alpine tradition and urban modernity of form and space. One does not have to go far to find examples in Gstaad. There is the Saanerslochbahn with its cable car station and the state-of-art gondolas which are faster, quieter and have more space. Jaggi won the Skiarea Test award for architecture 2019.

The Gstaad airport is another good example of their work with its visible beam structure of the roof open to view. Hotels too are included from the key project the Alpina to the Spitzhorn, Ermitage and Bernerhof. But renovation of chalets and new constructions are also top of their list.

"Of the three elements of architecture such as light, proportion and structure," said Elisabeth Wampfler, a co-partner in Jaggi, "I consider light the most important. It's natural, costs nothing and has a good effect on people. The use of glass is a cornerstone in the airport as the view onto the runway and the mountain is superb. But there is also functionality - how to park a helicopter and an aircraft in a building. The cableway station at the top of Saanersloch is site specific and is a

Saanerslochbahn with its cable car station.

good example of the fusion of alpine tradition of wood and urban modernity of glass."

The practice has an interdisciplinary team with over 30 years experience from the initial flash of inspiration to the delivery of the completed project. It consists of Elisabeth Wampfler and her partners, Urs Kunz in charge of the site management and Klaus Breuniger, interior designer. Their concern is to make their clients happy in their spaces and give the right answer to a question.

"It's incredible how life turns out because my dream was always to be at sea," she said with a smile. "I went to study architecture at EPFL in Lausanne. I liked living in the city and specialised in urban planning. But life conspired against me. A Gstaad architect Stephan Jaggi needed someone who spoke French for a big renovation of a chateau outside Lausanne. When the project was finished, I took on a few of his projects in the Saanenland. If it had just been to do chalets, I wouldn't have moved back. But I have had the incredible luck to work on some amazing, unusual projects here in the Saanenland."

Her favourite architectural firm is the Norwegian Snøhetta who designed the prize-winning National Opera and Ballet in Oslo. The building established intimate contact with the public as it gives the impression of a glacier emerging from a fjord. The flat roof is used as a square and is popular as the cafes and gift shop have access to the waterfront.

Elisabeth now lives in Saanen in the house she inherited from her grandmother. It was renovated with a new interior design and has a modern kitchen and bathroom. It's a far cry from the teenager who wanted a seafarer's career. But as she acknowledged, "I took a decision and have the responsibility for it," she said. "That's my philosophy."

Chaletbau Matti Architektur

Rotlistrasse 1
Tel 033 748 9010
info@chaletbaumatti.ch
www.chaletbaumatti.ch

Chaletbau Matti is the gold standard for luxury chalets in Switzerland. For almost 80 years, the company has focused on Swiss values, outstanding craftsmanship, precision and cutting-edge technology which is combined with top-notch design and a comprehensive range of services. Reclaimed, often very valuable old woods such as ornamental and support beams, wall coverings, roof trusses, etc. are processed in the carpentry workshop in Saanen and stored in the old wood warehouse in Château d'Oex. At the headquarters in Gstaad, the showroom is an experience in itself not only for the splendid high-tech display but it's an encyclopaedia of the materials available. Customers can look around in sample rooms and can admire showpieces from the 'Antiques Collection.'

"That's what our customers want - old values and the highest quality," said Daniel Matti, the CEO and third generation. "New chalets cost CHF 5 million and upwards. Someone once said that these chalets are the modern castles of the 21st century. From the outside you can see little or nothing, but the inner life is unique. The chalets are an expression of discretion. Behind the walls, however, there are parking halls, indoor swimming pools, entire cinemas or discos. The range of customer requests in interior design varies from a New York-style loft to an old farmhouse. For everyone of our craftsmen who work on the demands, it's a great challenge and satisfaction. We have the opportunity to realise something extraordinary with our clients which is not often found."

From the initial concept to the project planning, the land acquisition (if necessary) and the execution, the firm now offers its customers a complete package. They have 40 employees from the architecture, planning and design department and 70 specialists in the timber construction sector. Besides most of the prestigious chalets in Oberbort, a superb example of their public work is The Alpina Gstaad. They sourced and installed Ringgenberg limestone and antique barn wood as well as the centuries-old painted dressers and wardrobes.

"Some two-thirds of our work is building new chalets," he said, "and a third is renovations. But the rest is silence: names of customers are not mentioned, there's no information about locations and categories of luxury. Discretion is a prerequisite and a success factor for us. Therefore, both our staff and the outside contractors have to sign a confidentiality agreement. In internal training and workshops, the employees are also aware of the issue."

The firm was started in 1941 by Daniel's grandfather, Jakob, who was a carpenter and built simple chalets. (See entry, Cedric Notz). His father, Walter took over took over in 1968 when building regulations were stringent and he trained as a draughtsman and architect. Daniel studied Economics and Business Administration at St Gallen university and worked for PriceWaterhouse Coopers in real estate corporate finance after graduation. In 2010, he followed in his father's footsteps and took over the company.

"My philosophy is to strive for the best," he said. "You can always do better. You have to stay open-minded with no fixed ideas and look for opportunities. Above all, be true to yourself. I'm a hard working Swiss and I don't get ideas above my station because I'm working on a chalet worth CHF 10 million or more."

Armin Werren AG

Lauenenstrasse 76
Tel. 033748 8400
info@werrenag.ch
www.werrenag.ch

If you think that painting and plastering, staining and gilding are mundane tasks in building or renovating, think again. Armin Werren has turned them into exciting processes and even into forms of art. Another way of expressing it, is they beautify and protect building materials of all kinds with forms and colours that are encountered everyday at home and in public. They are masters of the profession of painting and plastering. Armin Werren AG is headed by Philippe Werren, Eric Werren and Stephan Bettler.

"The company was started some 55 years ago by my grandfather, Armin," said Philippe Werren, the third generation, "who painted houses inside and outside. Everyone first worked only in the summer and autumn and from Christmas until April they were ski instructors. They met future clients on the ski slopes. It was only in the 1980s that we worked the whole year and in 1986 my dad, Louis added plastering and other services."

Besides helping Daniel Matti's uncle, Peter and his wife Anita, with milking his cows and weeding in the alps in summer, there was another important job for Philippe. He and his younger brother Eric would clean all the tin cans which were sent by the hotels and

Seating round a swimming pool.

restaurants as they were used to store paint. Philippe served his apprenticeship with a small company in Bern and then did his national service. He became an officer and served an extra two years.

"I returned in 2000 to work at the family's company," he said. "My role is in the office as according to my parents, I was born with two left hands. I prefer to work wth excel sheets. Eric is the artist who even designs boardroom tables, Stephan supervises the projects and all three of us are involved in sales. I'm proud of what we do as we've returned to old techniques, using oil-based paints instead of acrylic and have employees who have worked for us for 40 years and are skilled in the old traditions. You just have to look at some buildings we've maintained like the Chesery, Hählen - Bed & Baby and on the Promenade, the Olden and Romang Shuhhaus."

Philippe's parents still live in the house which belonged to his grandparents and is next to the office buildings and workshop. Other families might have sold the land to build chalets but the Werrens are devoted to their business and to the welfare of their employees.

Louis Martin and his wife Elisabeth

CF Immobilier

Rougemont
Tel. 026 925 10 00
Gstaad Tel. 033 748 10 02
Chateau d'Oex Tel. 026 924 53 55
Bulle Tel. 026 921 05 05
www.cfimmobilier.ch

Louis Martin is one of the top Swiss experts in real estate sales to foreigners in Gstaad, Rougemont, Chateau d'Oex and Bulle. In addition, he has international exposure through his agency with Barnes. The price per metre varies from a high at Gstaad where the price is no limit and drops as you go down the valley. From CHF 20,000 upwards at Oberbort, Gstaad to Rougemont (CHF 10,000) and ultimately at Chateau d'Oex (CHF 6,000).

"We offer a concierge service to our clients such as opening the shutters, cleaning and filling the fridge," said Louis who has 30 years experience in real estate. "But each owner of a chalet or apartment is similar to operating a small to medium size enterprise (SME) because they use various services of the region such as a notary, artisans, furniture shops, restaurants and hotels, garage, gardener, housekeeping, hospital care, sports facilities, private schools, real estate agent, etc. My Barnes connection is important as a client might also want me to sell his property in Paris or New York."

Louis Martin grew up in Rougemont, a traditional village with a Cluny church. He gained a commercial diploma and during his apprenticeship worked at the MOB. His first job was with an insurance company (1987-1990). He changed to real estate in Chateaux d'Oex, acquired a Federal brevet in property and in 1996 bought the shares in CF Immobilier. As owners, he and his wife Elisabeth expanded into Rougemont, Gstaad and Bulle.

"I'm proud that we have 12 professional staff who can offer all facets of real estate from brokerage, sales, management, property administration, vacation rentals, promotion, project management," he said, "as well as complementary areas such as insurance, legal counsel, trustee and real estate appraisal."

He skis but his real passion is ice hockey which he has played as a junior. When he started, his large size and height was a disadvantage because smaller players would speed fast and run with the puck. However, the game has changed and the strategy is to have players his size who pass a lot and hit on others.

"The majority of buyers discover the resort during a holiday and then fall in love with the valley and start their research on the spot," he said. "I'm often asked what properties are most sought after by these clients. The answer is three bedroom apartments with a surface area of approximately 150 m2. Or old cottages to renovate."

Michael Tschanz

Tschanz Architektur AG

Waldmattenstrasse 5
CH-3778 Schönried
Tel. 033 744 41 42
info@tschanz-architektur.ch
www.tschanz-architektur.ch

Tschanz is an extraordinary architectural practice because of its wide-ranging expertise. They are longterm architects of the Palace hotel, have designed an industrial laundry, a youth centre, a triple gymnasium building, the new Romang shop and a chalet in the Promenade as well as renovation and construction of chalets.

"We've undertaken major projects

for the Palace hotel over the past 30 years," said Michael Tschanz, the second generation. "But what makes it challenging is that all work must be done between the peak seasons such as spring and autumn. When we built the Spa which is under the tennis courts we had to be innovative. The chimney of the fireplace couldn't come straight up so we had to run a horizontal air duct. An important feature of the spa was the wall made of natural stone from the Blausee."

Michael was born and educated in Gstaad. He served his apprenticeship for four years and it was followed by further studies in Bern. He joined his father Peter Tschanz at his practice in Schönried and his first big job was as a site manager in Saanen. He supervised the building of the large chalet Birdie with four floors and an underground level. He took over the practice from his father in 2010 and today has some eight staff.

"I was chuffed that the owner gave me the opportunity as I had to deal at first hand with all the artisans," he said, "and with the problems and issues as they arose. It's one thing to have a set of plans but another to implement them. Ever since I was a boy I was fascinated by the whole process of construction. I'm not the kind of person who wants to do nice drawings every day. I want to talk to the specialists like the carpenters, plasters, painters. They all are part of a team. Star architects only want do their own thing. But I start with a client. What they need. The size, the shape and the materials they want. They show me pictures with a lot of styles and materials and I narrow them down to something homogenous."

The new hotel laundry took Michael into the realm of high-tech. It's a milestone in terms of ecology, technology and business management. One of the innovations is the re-cycling of heat. Other projects include wooden buildings such as the multifunctional Youth Centre with a skate park and the triple sports hall for OSZ school and Gymnasium or complex jobs like the Palace Spa.

"My advice for young people," he said, "is to learn languages like English and French. It's not what you do later but it's very important being able to communicate."

Galler Schreinerei AG

Farbstrasse 78
Saanen
Tel. 0337441047
info@galler-ag.ch
www.w.galler-ag.ch

When it comes to carpentry, renovations and new buildings, Galler is a leading name in Gstaad. The company values both the old and the new, producing contemporary designs but also interiors in the traditional styles that have been around since Tom Galler's grandfather Paul founded the company over 60 years ago. Besides, the production and design of interiors,

Tom Galler

windows, doors, kitchens, furniture and repairs, a speciality is their work in old wood.

"As a master carpenter, I'm a perfectionist," said Tom, "because I work down to the last millimetre and refuse to be satisfied with anything else. To be a joiner you have to enjoy working with your hands and have a feeling for working with wood. I love the satisfaction you get seeing what you have created at the end of the day."

Tom left Gstaad to do his apprenticeship and later gained his masters. But when he left home, his father, Paul, told him not to join the firm until he was 30 to gain experience and learn from other companies. While based in Grindelwald and later in Bern and Seeland, he returned regularly to see his family.

"When I returned in 2011 after 13 years, the company had 20 workers," he said. "My grandfather started with three people and now we have between 25-30. I continued in the same vein as my father who always invested in modern technology and machinery. We have two CNC machines (computer numerical control) which enables the automated control of machining tools as well as many other high-tech machines."

"Although, technology is important, our

workers play a big role," he continued. "We are lucky to have several long-term employees that have been with us for over 40 years as well as second generation staff in our firm. It's still a family run company. My father is in the office, my mother who also runs a bookshop in Saanen does the payroll and my brother Marc who is part of carpenter team, is doing his foreman training. During the week we all have lunch together."

Saanenland comes with its own challenges and rewards. The client base is varied from locals who like traditional work to international clients who want something distinctive. The current trend of using old wood for interiors is very fashionable as it adds to the beauty of a chalet and unique character to a room. The downside is it's hard to obtain, costs a lot more than new wood and is labour intensive to work.

Some special projects have included the production of bullet-proof windows; doors that are almost 5m high to accommodate sculptures; the lining of a 46m tunnel between chalets with wooden panels for a long gallery to hang paintings; the fabrication of the rounded windows for the Saanen church; and the heli-transport of materials to hard-to-reach places like Geltenhütte at over 2,000m.

"There's a great local spirit among the community here," said Tom, "which makes living and working here so extraordinary."

Evolution of the Chalet in Saanenland

Here are two examples. The third is a masterpiece found in Saanen, the Jaggi Drogerie. (See entry, Introduction.)

1. Heidenhaus with Heiden wooden cross built in 1456 and is in Schibeweg, Gstaad. It's the oldest and simplest house in Bernese Oberland.

2. Reichenbach-Aellen Haus in Grubenstrasse in 1605. Here we have more writing, flowers and patterns on the exterior.

Heidenhaus with Heiden wooden cross.

Reichenbach-Aellen Haus.

Kinogässli
Senksäulen

Chapter 8. Farming

The 700 year-old tradition: Cows, goats and cheese.

The Agricultural Association of Saanenland represents the interests of some 200 members including a third who are bio farmers. The areas covered vary from cattle breeding and markets to agri-tourism and dairy farming which is the main occupation. An important ecological balance is maintained on each dairy farm. The cultivated land supports different animals such as deer and chamois, hares and many species of birds as well as orchids and gentian. The number of livestock on farms are limited to ensure no overexploitation of cultivated land and meadows.

Annual agricultural show.

Heidi Schopfer

Bergmatteweg 25
3777 Saanenmöser
Tel. 079 529 21 09
www.landwirtschaft-saanenland.ch

Heidi Schopfer and her husband Emil have been practicing organic farming through Bio Suisse since 1994. She is active on several fronts including the Gstaad Authentique (GA) products, on the local council for Saanenmõser and managing the office of the Agricultural Association of Saanenland.

"Regional products are increasing in popularity and are represented by Gstaad Authentique (GA)," she said. "In some cases, they are in even greater demand than organic products. In return for a small representation fee and a percentage of sales, GA provides additional marketing channels for meat, bread, eggs, milk and cream."

Heidi grew up in Lauenen in a poor family. Her grandfather, Albert Hefti, only had a herd of goats while her father owned eight cows and in winter was a wood cutter. Today, she and Emil make a renowned cheese called Isenau. From mid-June to the end of August, they make the delicious L'Etivaz cheese AOC, a hard cheese made from unpasteurised alpine milk produced on the Alp, above the wood fire according to the strict specifications of the L'Etivaz cooperative.

"At the time, you could make a living having only six to eight cows," she said, "Nowadays you need double to make ends meet which has resulted in fewer farmers. In 1993, there were 30 farmers in Saanenmöser while in 2018 there were only 17. We have 15 cows and produce between 300-400 round cheeses (each averaging 10 kgs) a year. My husband also works as an electrician."

Christoph Bach is the president of the Agricultural Association of Saanenland. He lives in Turbach and has herd of between 16 to 18 cows and seven pigs.

"Cheesemaking remains the main profitable activity for hundreds of years," he said. "The cows are herded up to the alpine pastures from mid-June until September. The herders are paid in kind e.g. eight to ten kgs of milk per cow. The cheese is still made in the traditional way of heating the milk in cauldrons and when the whey is separated from the curds, it's fed to the pigs. Some 300 tons of alp cheese is produced annually in the region."

The Agricultural Association of Saanenland celebrated its 100th anniversary in 2018. Over 120 Simmental cows were on display, some weighing a ton. An important event in the Saanen farmers' life is the annual cattle show at which the experts pick the most beautiful cow. There are four categories which include the general appearance, the legs and feet as well as the gait, the udders - their shape and the tits - the length and whether they are in the right position. Andre Marmet's cow Rahel is one such winner with 98%. It is eight years old and has produced six calves all females.

There are some 80 alpine working farms and about 200 dairies in Saanenland. Walter von Siebenthal and his daughter, Andrea Sprenger von Siebenthal are a good example of transhumance in Saunenmöser. For over centuries they have moved in summer over three levels from the valley (1,000m) to the voralp (1,500m) and finally to the Alp farm (1,800m)

"Until recently, the family was split during the summer with the mother and some children staying at the farm in the valley," said Walter von Siebenthal, "while the herd was taken up to the alps for eight to eleven weeks. Consequently, it was goats that provided the milk for them. Nowadays, the whole family goes up to the alp to make cheese."

Andre Marmet's cow Rahel.

The Bach family in Feutersoey epitomises the modern face of traditional dairy farming in Gstaad. Karin and her husband Ueli are well travelled - he went round the world twice as a young man and she always went abroad on family holidays. Later, she became a flight attendant for Swissair. They have three grown up daughters.

"I was born in Bern and raised near Zurich to the Fleuti family with no connections to agriculture," she said, "and for some 30 years I've been the wife of a dairy farmer and cheese maker on Gummalp during the summer season, one of the mountain pastures in the region.

In the summer, we have some 130 Simmental cows and about 60 heifers and calfs in the two Alpine huts. In the winter, the herd is reduced to about 30 animals since space and food is limited in the valley."

"My husband is also a passionate livestock trader," she continued. "For over 40 years he and his father had a cattle auction at the end of summer. He travels around Switzerland buying and fulfilling orders as he knows exactly what his customers want. Each cow's origins are well documented down the generations and even the date of the their transfer after a sale is noted."

The months of June, July and August

are spent up in the alps and are an intense time. Cheese making begins after the cows which have spent the night outside are herded inside the barn and milked at about 8am. The process is finished at around lunchtime and the same routine is continued every day including weekends. Sometimes they have to dash down to the valley for haymaking. It's hard physical work but also very fulfilling because they can see a result at the end of the day.

There was a gradual handover of the farm as for the last 20 years, her husband's parents retired and Karin and her husband took over the cheesemaking on Gummalp. During the three decades, Karin has become a connoisseur of alpine cheeses. From the taste and the aroma, she can tell the origin of cheeses because of the different vegetation on the alps.

"There are two sides of Gstaad and Saanenland - the locals who live here, the foreigners who have chalets or stay at one of the many exclusive hotels," she said. "However, there's a good balance between the farmers who survive on moderate incomes and the luxury that surrounds them. Both live in mutual respect and we aren't intimated by the celebrities nor their wealth because we understand that they too appreciate the authentic lifestyle and the beauty of the landscape."

Züglete, a term to describe the time when the cows return to valley from the alps on September 30.

Alpine Cheese Dairy Tours

The tours include cheese production, whey baths, restaurant and accommodation.
Here are several examples:

Vorder-Eggli Alp
By car from Saanen/Rübeldorf to Chalberhöni and dirt road to the Alp. Hiking trails also lead there.

Location
Helen and Ruedi Wehren Mobile: +41 79 380 73 05 or +41 79 257 22 76.

If you want to experience the authentic cheesemaker who goes back 20 generations, then Ruedi is your man. (See entry, Delice). He still uses the ancient equipment which includes the copper pot, the wooden hoist to hold the pot, the salt water to soak the cheese and the heavy stone press to push the cheese into the round form.

"I have 18 cows and normally I make cheeses during the summer season," he said. "The best cows are interbreeding between the Simmental and Holstein as you get good milk and good meat. They are known as Swiss Fleckvieh or SF."

Ruedi's cheese can only be bought at their farm or if you eat at the Kuuhl restaurant in Basel, they have the hobel cheese. See Ruedi in action on https://www.youtube.com/watch?v=8AOhvymcxhl

Turnels, Turbach Älplerzmorge,
Bathing in fresh whey, sleeping in a straw barn, direct sales of air-dried meat and Alpine cheese. (See entry, Anita Roth). Starting at the Wasserngrat railway valley station, after 100m turn right into a small road. This road leads through the valley up to the Alp. After walking for an hour and a half you will reach the Alp at 1,900m above sea level between Wasserngrat and Giferspitz.

Jakob Zumstein,
Mobile +41 79 635 96 87

Bodme, Gstaad.
Take the Wispile gondola to the middle station, then 10 minutes on foot. Or head for Berghaus Wispile and then follow the cheese trail to the Alp, around 1 hour on foot,

Dominik Matti,
Tel. +41 79 406 97 39

NB The tours are only offered in the summer and during the mornings.

Local Farm Products

Robert Aellen
Tromweg 19
Tel. 033 744 64 25
- Dried mutton
- Salsiz (sausage)
- Bratwurst sausage
- Traditional cheese

Stefan Addor
Untersattel
3782 Lauenen
Tel. 033 765 32 88
- Alpine and grated cheese
- Veal, Alpine pig and boar meat
- Eggs
- Dried sausage and air-dried meat

Ueli Bach–Reichenbach
Turbachstrasse 149
3781 Turbach
Tel. 033 748 15 23
- Alpine cheese and Hobelkäse
- Alpine pigs

Benjamin and Patricia von Grünigen
Aebnithus Gstaadstrasse 97
3780 Gstaad
Tel. 033 33 744 18 79/079 611 17 81
- Alpine cheese
- Tea
- Jams
- Dried sausage
- Pear bread

Christian and Christa Hefti
Gsteigstrasse 40
Tel. 033 744 90 28/079 611 17 81
- Beef and veal
- Dried sausage and air-dried meat
- Alpine cheese and Hobelkäse
- Raclette cheese in autumn and winter
- Hen and ostrich eggs
- Farm-bred ostrich meat
- Empty ostrich eggs (decoration)
- Pasta
- Meringues
- Liqueurs
- Dried ostrich necks for dogs

Chapter 9. Entertainment

Anyone for tennis, polo? What about country or classical music?

Menuhin Festival

Gstaad Menuhin Festival & Academy
Dorfstrasse 60
3792 Saanen
Tel. 033 748 8338
info@gstaadmenuhinfestival.ch
www.gstaadmenuhinfestival.ch

Gstaad Menuhin Festival is one of the best in Switzerland if not Europe. It's a cornucopia of music and runs for about seven weeks with about 70 performances in summer. Christoph Müller is the artistic director of the festival which was founded by the violinist Yehudi Menuhin in 1957. One of the innovations is the Neeme Jãrve prize for conducting which is organised by Gstaad Menuhin Festival Academy.

"I've been attending the concerts for the past 35 years," said Denise Elfen, a resident of Gstaad. "It's unique because of the variety of concerts from classical to folk and contemporary music. The

Christoph Müller

venues are also a great attraction particularly the beautiful churches such as the medieval Saanen with its 500 year old paintings, Le Temple de Vers l'Eglise with its five sided choir and five windows as well as Zweisimmen, Lauenen and Gsteig."

"But what is outstanding is the Neeme Jãrve prize for conducting," she

The set for Bizet's *Carmen* was designed by Aline Foriel-Destezet.

continued. "I listened to 12 musicians conducting the same composition with the same orchestra and it was proof that a conductor can make or break a composition. If he's good it's reflected in the music but if not, the composition can result in a poor performance."

The President of the Menuhin is Aldo Kropf, the Artistic Director is Christoph Müller and the President of the Friends is Caroline Schwenter.

"The Menuhin Festival is the main event in Saanenland's annual calender," said Aldo Kropf, who is its president. "It has reached a high quality and it's my duty to maintain that standard. The founder, Yehudi Menuhin, was keen on music in churches and we have carried out his wishes as the main part of the festival happens there."

Christoph Müller is a top impresario aka multitasking musical manager in Switzerland. He has taken the Gstaad Menuhin Festival from the brink of extinction to a world class festival in Europe. He revived the Paul Sacher's Basel Chamber Orchestra which had given its last concert in 1987 and renamed it the "Kammerorchester Basel" in 1999 and thirdly, he is a co-founder of Swiss Classics, a company of music management and gives performances as the Lucerne Chamber Circle since 1999/2000.

"My theme for the 64th edition in 2020 is "Wien," said Christoph, the enthusiastic and talented musician. "In 2018, my festival-theme turned around "the Alps," what a popular subject! It ranged from Brahms' '1st Symphony which was written in Thun, Strauss' Alpine.

Symphony, to the two Swiss symphonies by Mendelssohn - all works with a strong thematic relevance. What set the tone was the fascinating forces of nature and the powerlessness man has felt against the mountains and valley."

Christoph was born in Basel and grew up in the region in the village, Möhlin, close there, in Muttenz, he graduated with a Matura. He had a talent for music and studied at the Bern conservatory majoring in cello. He also gained diplomas for orchestra and concert (1991-1998). Once he graduated, he played in various chamber music ensembles and won different awards including the Bank Association Culture Prize 1996. He is a founding member of the Trio con Brio with whom he produced a CD at the label Gallo (Lausanne).

"There were two highlights which I was proud of," he said. "The first was when the star orchestra, the London Symphony orchestra, came to Gstaad and brought glamour with it. The second was to introduce famous soloists such as Cecilia Bartoli, Nigel Kennedy, Jonas Kaufmann and Alfred Brendel, idols whose very presence caused excitement. To achieve softness in playing, sometimes Brendel swathed his fingers in bandages. But we've always stuck to the formula of three pillars. The first is chamber music in beautiful churches. The second is symphonic concerts in the specially constructed tent with the most modern and technical acoustic standards. The third is to present inspired music whether its jazz/classical or tangos with an accordion mixed with Vivaldi's Seasons."

Each season Christoph starts with a white page and it's a challenge to create something amazing and original. But he started from zero after Yehudi Menuhin's chosen successor the Latvian violinist Gidon Kremer had the wrong formula for the festival which caused it almost to go bankrupt. He was 30 when he applied for the position and the 11 member of the council took a courageous decision to employ a greenhorn. What Christoph had to do was to closely connect with the Menuhin spirit but add new content.

"My music moment occurred when I was on holiday in the Valais," he said. "I was around 6 years old and I heard the famous cellist Pierre Fournier playing in the old church in Ernen a suite from Bach. It was then that I decided to become a professional musician. We ended up in the music village of Ernen because my parents were music lovers."

"My philosophy is to find an internal voice which tells you what's the ambition of your life," he said. "Another important aspect is to be creative as it keeps you alive. I was fortunate to find my own way through my internal voice and my parents who supported me."

The people of Saanenland have taken the Menuhin Festival very much to their hearts, but specially the Menuhin Festival Friends. Everyone is welcome and there are some 200 members who pay CHF 2,200 a year and receive two tickets for four concerts each year in the tent . They also are invited to dinner at the partner hotel Ermitage of the Gstaad Menuhin Festival and the Palace. But the greatest excitement and pleasure are the seven weeks of concerts when they can hear world class orchestras and artists like Jonas Kaufmann or Sol Gabetta.

"I had the chance of meeting Yehudi Menuhin when I first came to Gstaad," said Caroline Schwenter, President of the Friends. "It was a magical moment."

Caroline is from Bern where she trained as a radiographer at the Insel hospital. She married a local man, Jürg Schwenter, and together with her husband they run a paint and plastering business. They have three children. In addition, as she has a great interest in the history of Saanen and the surrounding region, she is a local guide of Gstaad-Saanenland.

The Gstaad Academy offers a range of master classes for young professionals as well as orchestra courses that are aimed at amateur players of all ages.

"My work is exciting as I have to juggle the different masterclasses at the same time," said Lukas Wittermann, manager of the academy project, "and also organise the rehearsals for the Gstaad Festival Orchestra and the Youth orchestra. They are composed of professional musicians and youth amateurs from 13-18."

Lukas is a German cellist who lives with his wife, a flutist, in Feutersoey next to a barn with cows. He is responsible for the five sections of the academy: the piano, the strings, the vocals, the baroque and the conducting. "One of my memorable experiences since I've come to Switzerland has been to listen to Maurice Steger on the recorder and the Catalan soprano, Nuria Rial. It was like listening to a twittering of two birds."

Sommets Musicaux de Gstaad

Cour de Saint-Pierre 5
1204 Geneva
Tel. 022 738 6675
www.sommets-musicaux.com

Since its creation in 2001, the Festival of Musical Summits of Gstaad has become a prestigious winter event for all lovers of classical music. Every year for nine days, young talents, chamber orchestras, internationally renowned artists delight audiences from Switzerland and abroad.

The Festival is organized around three pillars: three cycles of concerts in three

Renaud Capuçon

exceptional places. In the afternoon, the Gstaad Chapel gives pride of place to a promising youth with a series of concerts honouring a particular instrument. In the evening, the churches of Rougemont and Saanen treat the public to outstanding soloists and orchestras of international stature.

Renaud Capuçon is the artist director who creates a programme that is in keeping with the tradition of earlier editions and meets the budget. He is a violinist and also the founder and artistic director of the Aix en Provence Easter Festival.

"My job as Artistic Director is to assemble musicians with very different outlooks," he said, "to offer the audience a highly varied group of artists: young ones who are still unknown but are very soon about to become very much more so, big stars like Radu Lupu or Nelson Freire, and musicians from my generation like Nicholas Angelich."

"I serve the audience and composers like Bach by playing them in harmony with the other musicians," he continued. "Some classical stars like to shine over the composer and give their version of the piece. But they tend to have big egos and I feel they do a disservice to music as a whole. For me, the music brings so much joy particularly through coordination of the whole orchestra."

The festival is an important winter event, the exceptional meeting between the artists, a music-loving public and the partners of the Festival. It compliments the summer Menuhin Festival.

"The idea for the festival originated when I got to know Thierry Scherz in 1998," said Ombretta Ravessoud, the co-founder. (See entry, Ravessoud). "We agreed to have a cultural event in winter and the Scherz family and the Gstaad Palace were involved from the start in 2001. For example, we always organise dinners in the Salle Baccarat with the artists and the audience after the concerts. Some of artists also stay at the Palace."

"Is there anything more magical than listening to a classical concert virtually among friends in local churches?" she asked, "after a day on skis? Lastly, there are two prestigious awards."

The Prix Thierry Scherz is sponsored by the Fondation Pro Scientia et Arte and the Friends of the Sommets Musicaux de Gstaad. It represents an opportunity to recognize one young virtuoso and offer them encouragement by giving them the chance to record a debut CD with orchestra for the Claves Records SA label.

The Prix André Hoffmann, an endowment of CHF 5,000 is awarded for the best interpretation of a work. It also provides the support that enables the Festival to host the composer in residence for the entire week of the event.

Pierre Dreyfus is the president of "Les Amis des Sommets Musicaux de Gstaad" and Vice Chairman of the Dreyfus & Sons Bankers in Basel. He has been interested in music from an early age when he learnt the piano. He grew up and studied in Paris. As a teenager, he played the electric organ in a pop group. He gained a degree in civil engineering and an MBA at INSEAD, and his first job was in a construction company. He has two children.

"One of the key projects was the runway at the airport in Curacao, the Dutch West Indies," he said. "Later, I started my own film production company and one of my major clients was Canal+. At the age 45, I joined my father in the family bank in Basel."

"I had often come to concerts at the Menuhin Festival and the Sommets de Musicaux de Gstaad," he said. "In 2018, I was offered to become president of the Friends of the Sommets Musicaux de Gstaad. It is now a great pleasure to work with the team which consists of Vera Michalski-Hoffmann, Ombretta Ravessoud, the ambitious and talented artistic director Renaud Capuçon and many other wonderful people. My task consists mainly to extend the great family of music lovers and raise more funds to ascertain the continuation of the festival."

Gstaad New Year Music Festival
Princess **Caroline Murat** is the artistic director and founder of the Gstaad New Year Music Festival which is under the patronage of H.S.H Prince Albert II of Monaco. She is an important figure in the music world and for the past three decades, under her stage name, Caroline Haffner, she performed in concert halls around the world. In Switzerland, for example, she founded two other music festivals.

She was a child prodigy and when she won first prize at the Geneva International Competition she was hailed as the new Martha Argerich. Even the Russian cellist Mstislav Rostropovich complemented her on her piano playing. She met him during a master class when she was a piano accompanist. He suggested they play something together and they performed one of Mozart's Four Hands pieces. He also took an interest in her career.

"I was the only child and I was forced to like music by my mother, Martha," she said with a sardonic smile. "At the head of my bed was a death mask of Beethoven and every morning I had to listen to a movement of Beethoven. But I had my fun too as I stood in front of the mirror conducting and dreamt of leading an orchestra. Then at the age of seven to my mother's delight it was discovered that I had a special talent for the piano. And unfortunately my life changed as I had to stay at home to practice while other kids enjoyed themselves. At nine, I entered the Paris conservatoire with a special authorisation and left with a licence de concert at 14 which was presented to her by the famous conductor Charles Munch. I won two scholarships, one to the Soviet Union through my teacher Lev Oborin and then a Fulbright. I had played before Eunice Kennedy Schriver when her husband was the American Ambassador in Paris and she arranged that I could go the Julliard School in New York."

"When I was 17, I experienced the demanding life of a musician when I went on a tour of Spain," she continued. "I toured for 28 days out of the 30 with concerts all over the country. In most of the places, there were only rudimentary facilities not

Caroline Murat

even television. I was relieved when I finally arrived in Madrid and looked forward to dinner at the Ambassador's home. But by then I was so exhausted that I collapsed without any food."

Princess Caroline was born in Paris as her father, Prince Jerome was a direct descendant of Napoleon through the emperor's younger sister Caroline who married his Marshal Joachim Murat. Her father taught her that the title does not offer rights but confers duties. Her mother was proud of her ancestry as she could trace her family back to the Haffner mayor of Salzburg. He was a patron of Mozart and for whom the composer wrote the Haffner Symphony and the Hafner Serenade. She married at 20 and has three children. Caroline travelled extensively with her banker husband and settled in different places such as Saudi Arabia, Barcelona, Madrid, Amsterdam, Casablanca, Montevideo, Buenos Aires and Monaco where she lived in a hôtel particulier which had frescoes by Paul Gervais. Although, she was no longer active as a concert pianist, she co-founded with Martin Engstroem the Verbier Festival academy. When Barbara Hendricks, his wife visited Monte Carlo she was able to help raise funds for it.

9

"The greatest thing is that there are people who continue to sincerely love music," she said. "They do so without regret or with a search for fame. They're not concerned that other musicians achieve success with all its trappings. There are only a few of them but believe me they do exist and continue to serve music. I experienced this as a 15 year old when I played to wounded soldiers for the Red Cross. There was a young, handsome man lying face down as he was shot in his back. I was playing Chopin and he was listening. From that day on, I told myself that my music would serve to alleviate pain, to raise people over it and give consolation. And I would try whole heartedly to give generously. Music is generosity."

A music lover, Daniel Aghion has remarked of her playing: "She has energy in her playing and literally tears the piano apart. It's gut-wrenching, it cannot leave you indifferent."

Country Night Gstaad

Le Chalet
Tel. 0337484487
info@countrynight-gstaad.ch
www.countrynight-gstaad.ch

Country night is one of the most renowned festival in Europe. The vision was to make it accessible to all from truck drivers to billionaires and offer a lineup of the top American artists. Consequently, the programme has included Emmylou Harris, Miranda Lambert, Kenny Rogers, Lady Antebellum and Ronan Keating and many more. Keating came just to sing a duet with LeAnn Rimes and left. However two years later he was the headliner.

"Country Night requires us to go to Nashville to sign up country and western singers for our programme," said Heidi Raaflaub, the event manager. "We go in November for the Country Music Association (CMA) awards show when outstanding artists are selected. The artists that impressed me most was the Midland, a Texan band that not only had presence but interacted well with the audiences."

Marcel Bach who runs the festival has a passion for country and western music. Right from the start Loretta Lynn and Conway Twitty appeared on the stage.

SPORTS

Hublot Polo Gold Cup Polo Club

Gstaad Lauenenstrasse 18,
PO-BOX 419
Tel 033 744 07 40
info@pologstaad.ch
www.polo-gstaad.ch

Since the inception of the Polo Gstaad in 1996, polo has been a beloved local tradition in the Saanenland. During the tournament which takes place every year in mid-August at the Gstaad airport, sporty Argentinian horses chase across the field.

Four teams compete, Hublot, Banque Eric Sturdza, Clinique La Prairie and Gstaad Palace. The best handicap is 10 while the worst is 0.

Pierre Genecand checking the course with polo players.

"Our aim is to give our guests an exceptional experience while also giving visitors the possibility to watch the games for free," said Pierre Genecand, president of the Hublot Polo Gold Cup. "The VIP tent now serves up to 500 lunches each day, and some 500 guests have been invited to the gala evening. Gourmet chefs prepare all the food." (See entry, Who's Who)

The Hublot Polo Gold Cup Gstaad is unique in the Swiss sports calendar that goes beyond the competition: a stunning setting among alpine peaks, an airport that becomes a polo club for a single weekend, exhibitors with original luxury products to discover, a playground for children during the weekend, a picturesque animation in the streets of Gstaad with the parade of teams. A different way to live polo at high altitude!

J. Safra Sarasin Swiss Open Gstaad

Neueretstrasse 2
PO Box 17
3780 Gstaad
Tel.+41 (0) 33 748 08 60
gstaad@gcmsa.ch
www.swissopengstaad.ch
www.jsafrasarasinswissopengstaad.ch

The J. Safra Sarasin Swiss Open Gstaad is over a century old and in 1915 was launched as the Alpine Wimbledon. It's

Federer serving.

an Association of Tennis Professionals tournament, ATP 250, which offers 250 points to a winner - others offer 500 or 1,000 points. However, it has seen the likes of the top Australians such as Roy Emerson and Margaret Smith Court, Stan Wawrinka and Roger Federer with whom Gstaad has a special relationship. The tournament's motto is "today's champions meet the stars of tomorrow." In 1998, Federer played his first ATP tournament in Gstaad and also received his first wild card. Dominique Thiem, the Austrian player who has a ranking of No 4 in the ATP was another player who received his wild card in Gstaad.

"My appearances at Gstaad in 2003 and 2004, when I arrived as Wimbledon champion were crazy," Federer told Adrian Ruch in an interview. "The media reported on my daily routine. What's Roger doing on Monday? What's Roger doing on Tuesday? People even wanted to know whether I eaten croissant or muesli for breakfast. They were surreal weeks."

Well, he went for a husky ride on a glacier and milked a cow so expertly that he received one, Juliette, as a gift. She produced alp cheese for him every year. Later, another cow followed, Désirée which was given by Ueli Bach in 2013. (See entry, farming). But perhaps, it provided much needed consolation as he lost the final 3-6,4-6 because of back pain.

"I was proud he participated in 2013 and brought his wife Mirka and the twin daughters," said Heidi Raaflaub, member of the tournament administration for over 10 years. "It was the twins' fourth birthday which was celebrated at the top of Eggli."

Some 30,000 spectators attend the oldest major tennis tournament in Switzerland which is held in the last week of July every year on clay. The ATP 250 in Gstaad is unique as it's the only one in the world that takes place in a small mountain village.

Jeff Collet who is the tournament director of the event is a keen sportsman. He practices several sports including golf, skiing, tennis, running and fitness. His formula for success is to discover something that you can do with passion and not just for money. This has led to being the official agency of the Alinghi Team, twice winner of the America's Cup, the Davis Cup and other major events.

Eagle Ski Club

Bissedürrigweg 18
Tel. 033 7484232

A crowning glory of Gstaad is the Eagle Club which is situated at the summit of the Wasserngrat and is reached by a chairlift which belongs to the club. The Eagle has over the past six decades had many illustrious members and unbridled wealth and celebrity status certainly helps to be invited to join. Former presidents have included the Earl of Warwick, Count Edouard Decazes, Prince Nicolas Romanoff and Urs Holder. The current president is Loula Chandris.

Members and guests are offered a level of privacy that they need to enjoy times with friends and family. Besides being a place to lunch in the company of like-minded people, members can take part in club races against such rivals as the equally exclusive the Caccia in Rome or the Racquet club and the Knickerbocker in New York.

Benoît d'Azy of the Corviglia club was the first secretary and introduced various rules. One of them which is part of the constitution is the limitation of the number of members of different nationalities and flags are flown to show which nationals are in residence.

The secretariat which consists of several staff members are treated like an extended family. Marianne Matti, for example, has been at the Club for over 22 years. She was born and educated

in Gstaad and her family coat of arms dates back to the 14th century. Her father and grandfather had connections with the Gstaad butcher shop. "The Club is looked upon by members as a home from home," she said.

The Eagle Ski Club organises numerous Club races in winter which are sponsored by members. In addition, the Eagle hosts two Interclub races, one for the teams of the Rosey, JF Kennedy schools and Eagle children and one for teams of distinguished Clubs from Rome, NY, the Hague, London, Paris and South America. It also hosts a race open to Saanenland residents and which formerly was always won by local racers. Lately the Eagle racers have been a match for them. In addition, the Taki and Jones Trophies are awarded to the fastest winter and summer climbs up to the clubhouse.

The Eagle was founded in 1957 by 81 members including the 8th Earl of Warwick, one of the most prestigious titles in the peerages of the UK. The Earl's father once remarked of their ancestral home, Warwick castle, which was sold to Madame Tussaud. "It stinks of old shoes, old socks and wet macintoshes." The 8th earl had enjoyed an acting career before the war under the screen name of Michael Brooke. His Hollywood career peaked in 1937, when he was given a role supporting Errol Flynn and David Niven in Dawn Patrol.

Eagle Ski Club.

Gstaad Yacht Club

Untergstaadstrasse 15
Tel 033 748 0190
Restaurant
Tel. 033 744 2825
www.gstaadyachtclub.com

The Gstaad Yacht Club (GYC) is in the centre of the village. When one would expect to see a harbour with sailing boats not far away, this club goes against the grain as the nearest body of water is over 50 km away at Lake Thun. This was the point raised by H.M. King Constantine of Greece, the patron of the GYC: "Let's create a global Yacht Club far away from waters instead of another local Club by the waters." Now after 20 years of existence, the GYC is flourishing with over 400 members from some 30 nationalities.

Every year in March, selected sailing clubs from different continents are invited to the Ski-Yachting in Gstaad, where a regatta is organized with model boats in the indoor pool after a ski race in the Bernese Oberland.
In October, the GYC organizes the Centenary Trophy in conjunction with the Les Voiles de Saint-Tropez, a regatta in which only a 100-year old boats and over can register. The winner in 2018 for the second time in a row, was the German brigade sloop Tilly XV, which was built in 1912 for Prince Henry of Prussia, the brother of Emperor Wilhelm II.
Since 2004, GYC Sports Members represent Switzerland at the Olympic Games. Besides Swiss, there are other

The Gstaad Yacht Club (GYC).

nations' members in the club too who all generously support the GYC Racing Team privately. The next teams are preparing for Tokyo 2020. With the Swiss- Belgian, Nils Theuninck in the Finn (Bronze U23 World Champion 2019) and Swiss-Spanish Mateo Lanz Sanz on the RS:X Windsurf (Swiss sailor of the year and Vice World Champion 2017) - the athletes' backgrounds are as international as the entire GYC membership.

In 2019, the elected board included Manrico Iachia (Commodore), Alejandro Dahlhaus (Rear Commodore), Morten Kielland (Sailing Officer), Christine Lang-Camerana (Social Events Officer) and Cindy Schönrich (Managing Director), among other members. (See separate entries, Iachia and Camerana.)

"When I was interviewed by the former Commodore, I confessed that I wasn't a great swimmer," said Cindy Schönrich, a charming woman. "He smiled at me and told me not to worry as sailors are on the water not in the water."

Born in Germany and after graduating from Thuringia business school and University in Ravensburg, Cindy worked at Messe Frankfurt, the world's second largest trade fair, congress and event organiser. When she joined the GYC in 2009, she brought her business and

Cindy Schönrich

organisational skills to the club. She is an ambassador for the GYC with international connections to clubs, promoters, yacht and boat owners, partners and sponsors.

"I came from a company where I had a very active social life to a club which makes social life a profession," she said. "In Gstaad, I also became more sportive and was taught sailing on Lake Thun. Now, I live in the countryside where cows graze outside my window. With a work integrated life, I still get the chance to travel sometimes between the summer and winter seasons."

The GYC so far has realised 30 official reciprocity agreements around the world. From the Yacht Club of Greece to Yacht Club de Santos (BRA), St. Francis Yacht Club (USA), the Royal Thames Yacht Club (UK), Royal Swedish Yacht Club, Royal Cape Yacht Club (SA), the Royal Hong Kong Yacht Club (HK) and the Royal Melbourne Yacht Squadron (AUS).

Hügelstrasse
COLNAGO
COLNAGO

Roeckl

Chapter 10. Schools

Local yokel or exclusive JFK education.

Interlaken Gstaad branch

Rumpleregässli 12
3780 Gstaad
Tel. 033 8281639
www.gyminterlaken.ch

In the Bernese Oberland, it's not unusual to find a branch of a top school located in a village. It saves the students time (up to four hours in this case) to travel to the nearest gymnasium and back.

"So instead of the students travelling to attend, we create a branch in the village," said Christoph Däpp, the headmaster of Gymnasium Interlaken branch. "It's the teachers who have to travel and 12 of the 17 of the staff teach in Interlaken and in Gstaad. But it's worthwhile because of the ease of attendance at the gymnasium enables students to go onto university. Nevertheless, only some 12% of the local children take this opportunity, the others choose an apprenticeship ."

Christoph Däpp who is a molecular biologist, first trained as a physical education teacher. Later, he gained a PhD through a dissertation on gene expression in skeletal muscles. His research studied simulated walking upwards and walking downwards and the effect on human muscle.

"In the last decade as headmaster, there are two events which I am proud of," he said. "The first is the establishment and refinement of the branch which is akin to applying for a grant because of all the work involved. The second is networking regionally for the students. It involves reaching out to artists, musicians and poets who can come and give talks at the Gymnasium. Of course, the important sporting events is the friendly competition of ski racing and ice hockey with Le Rosey."

For students who want to pursue a sports career or become professionals, the gymnasium can accommodate them. It means that they have to make-up the lost time through intensive studying. In the case of skiing, they are away for 45% of the time during the winter term. But the skilift is located nearby so they can spend maximum time on the slopes and still pursue their education. Talk about benefits children get in Gstaad!

OSZ Gstaad

Secondary school
Partner school
Swiss SKI

Rumplergässli 8
Tel 033 744 9429
www.http://www.schulen.saanen.ch/de/schule/volksschulen/gstaadosz

The local school system offers a comprehensive selection from kindergarten, primary, special needs school, secondary school to a gymnasium. The kindergarten/primary and the special needs schools are located at:

Gsteigstrasse 11
Tel .033744 2004

The Secondary school aka Oberstufingzetrum (OSZ) has pupils from ages of 13 to 15/16 years.

Martin Stãhli who is the headmaster, studied teaching in Bern and first came to Saanen in 1992 where he taught at the Primary school. In 2014, he was appointed headmaster of OSZ.

"Besides the ski training, I have encouraged talent by adding music classes," said Martin. "My aim for students who graduate from the school is for them to be self-confident and independent. That is how they can make a mark in the world. A former student, Florence Schindler, for example, is a hockey professional in Sweden."

John F. Kennedy International School

Chilchgasse 2
Saanen
Tel. 41 33 744 1372
ïnfo@jfk
www.jfk.ch

JFK is an English language international boarding and day school for 60 to 70 students between 5 and 14. Main features include a good preparation for secondary schools, small classes, English-as-a-second-language programmes, daily French classes, a family-like atmosphere and an excellent offering of sports and activities including daily skiing in winter. Henri Behar is the school director.

Institut Le Rosey

Winter campus January-March
Chalet Rex
3780 Gstaad
Tel. 033 748 0600
www.rosey.ch

"The story about the Gstaad campus began in 1915," said Christophe Gudin, the fifth Director-General in the school's history. "Due to the war, some of the students couldn't go home so Henri Carnal brought them to Gstaad. It was sunny up there and the students also learnt to ski. When

Henri suggested that they also had a term on the mountains, his father, Paul, went ballistic. 'What will we gain by having our students among the stupid peasants?' Henri was insistent that it would be a change from the wet, misty gloomy weather in Rolle. In the end his father agreed and since 1916, we've had a winter campus in Gstaad."

But it was a big undertaking and virtually everything had to be moved from furniture to bedding, stationery to office and sports equipment as well as personal belongings. A special train was hired which had to make several trips to accomplish the task. The tradition is still carried on today.

"I spent from zero to 18 years at Le Rosey," said Christophe. "I remember special moments at the Gstaad campus. There was a bakery/delicatessen at the bottom of the little alleyway that leads from Chalet Rex onto the Promenade. But it was out of bounds. So was it was fun to sneak there and buy little breads. Unfortunately, it doesn't exist."

Christophe learnt to ski at the age of three on his mother's feet at Wispile. It's Gstaad's local mountain and popular with families. He was in the ski team throughout his schooling. They trained every day in all weathers. Then once a year they competed against the local ski team from the Gymnasium.

"A memorable event for me was the symbolic walk to celebrate the 100th anniversary of the campus at Gstaad," he said. "We walked from the girl's campus at Schõnried to Gstaad at the end of the winter term. Some 400 Roséens and their teachers made their way down in a long snaking line and in excellent spirits."

Christophe completed his baccalaureate at Le Rosey and excelled in his studies. He gained a Master of Science at EPFL and while there was an exchange student at Carnegie Mellon University. It was followed by an MBA at INSEAD, Singapore. He joined McKinsey & Company as an Associate and 10 years later returned to Le Rosey where he was appointed director in 2015.

"There are multiple things that make Le Rosey unique," said Christophe. "One of them is that the school has two campuses. Lessons finish by lunchtime so the students can hit the slopes in the afternoon. Another feature is the Rosey 'Long weekend' in February which is an age-old school tradition bringing together Roseans, parents and some 800 - 1,000 anciens who attend academic meetings and enjoy sporting and social events over three intense days. There is a range of competitions, including curling, cross-country skiing and even backgammon."

The school was founded in 1880 by Paul Carnal. Philippe Gudin, the owner and the fourth director, shifted towards the arts and commissioned the Paul and Henri Carnal Hall from Bernard Tschumi which was built in 2014.

60
ENTEN-EDITION
ENTEN-EDITION
VERHEXT!
OMG

L/R Amalia Coulter (11) and Ciara Coulter (10) at the Rütti School Gstaad.

Chapter 11. Guides

She, a former flight attendant guides locally and he, a mountain guide who climbed the Eiger and is renowned for off-piste skiing.

Guides Gstaad-Saanenland

Rüttistrasse 10
Tel. 0796500278
www.guides-gstaad.ch

Anita Roth-Reuteler who was a former flight attendant and flew internationally now heads the Guides Gstaad-Saanenland who cater to the needs of visitors. There are 10 guides of different skills from the sporty ones who ride e-bikes or do hikes to others who can show the sights from the horse-driven carriages. But they are all full of anecdotes and stories from the history of the region.

Anita was born in Gstaad and her grandfather was the Charly who bequeathed his name to the tea-room.

Anita Roth-Reuteler

It was a local heritage as the first films were shown there and the place where couples tea-danced. Her father, René, like her grandfather, Charly, were pastry chefs and Stefan Romang who now runs R-Chocolate boutique was an apprentice there. (See entry, Stefan Romang).

Anita is affable, knowledgeable and fun. Climbing Kilimanjaro was on her bucket list which she ticked and is a plant expert as she trained as a herbalist. She is proud of her family, Reuteler, which dates back 1420 and wears a signet ring of their coat of arms. (See entry, farming).

"As my father cooked our meals, I didn't realise as a girl that it was normal for women to cook in the kitchen," she said with a smile. "A nice outing is to eat outdoors on a special caquelon table which is found in different parts of the region."

Ueli Hauswirth Mountain Guide

Mountain Guide member of Swiss Alpine Club.

Mattenstrasse 76
Tel. 079 211 2788
hauswirths@bluewin.ch

Ueli Hauswirth is a tough guy with a solid physique of a special ops soldier. He is someone you would trust in a tight spot in the mountains or off-piste. He grew up in Lauenen as a son of farming family. As a boy he had no skis and instead used wooden planks. Later, he had skis with metal edges. His mother improved them through painting the bottom with red paint to obtain a smooth surface and to steer them better. He once broke his leg as the bindings were little metallic boot holders with long leather straps with which the leather shoes were tied to the skis.

"My advantage over other mountain guides is that I'm prepared to travel according to the clients' wishes," said Ueli Hauswirth. "Other guides at resorts such as Grindelwald or Zermatt tend to stay put. For example, I have clients who are passionate about ski touring and as soon as the snow starts to melt in lower regions like here in Gstaad, we go ski touring to other, higher areas in Switzerland and all over the Alps from Nice to Salzburg where there's still snow."

He became an apprentice carpenter between 16-19 and joined the youth organisation of the Swiss Alpine Club (SAC). In 1978, he became a ski teacher and in two years later finished his course as a mountain guide.

"My proudest moment was when I graduated in 1980," he said. "A week later I guided my first client to the Eiger via the east-ridge the so-called Mittellegigrat. Then in 1981, I was hired by family to ski with them every winter and I still go ski touring with them. Since then, I have many regular clients in summer and winter with whom I share countless, unforgettable experiences in the mountains."

He recommends an easy summit with a spectacular view over the Alps from Mont Blanc to the Eiger. It's the climb of the 3'210m Sommet des Diablerets in the Glacier 3000 region with a mountain guide. The outing involves a glacier walk of about 1 hour and 30 min up to the summit.

Caquelon table to eat fondue in the open.

For rock climbers, we have lots of small climbing walls around the Saanenland and of course, the best known large climbing areas like Gastlosen and Sanetsch.

He is also member of the Swiss Alpine rescue team (ARS) and married to Christa is a local high flyer who now is the manager of Charly's. She was born in Gstaad and her father, Walter Baumer, was the concierge at the Bellevue hotel for 35 years. (See entry, Sonnenhof).

"When I started as an apprentice in real estate, I'd show the apartments to clients," she said. "One day, I took Julie Andrews to see an apartment in Rougemont and I was nervous because I wasn't sure where it was. But she reassured me and said we'd find it definitely. We did but she wasn't interested. At home, I'd been taught not to make a fuss when we'd see famous people in the village. Just treat them respectfully as they want their peace and quiet."

She is a ski instructor and met her husband, Ueli Hauswirth, while rock climbing. They have two daughters, Tanya and Natalie, both of whom are good skiers. Tanya won a trophy in the Eagle Ski Club competition. (See entry, Eagle Ski Club).

A guide for hiking, trekking and snowshoeing. Contact:

Hählen AG - Bed & Baby,
Gsteigstrasse 3,
Tel. 0337441327

Chapter 12. Photo Competition

People from all walks of life, locals and foreigners from 17-71 participated in a photo competition.

The results of the winners were glorious.

Photo by Evelyne Peten, the winner of Photo Competition.

Photo competition was organised to give locals as well as foreigners an opportunity to participate at first hand in the region they live in and love. The response was good as the people were from all walks of life, from different ages (16-71) and backgrounds (from students, chefs, veterinarians, farmers, carpenters, sports teachers, landscape gardeners, notary, medical doctor, member of the Eagle Ski Club, housewife, bank trainee, a potter, architect and pensioner.

Judges

The judges who live locally are a top international fine art photographer (Irene Kung), a world class gallerist (Patricia Low) and the local publisher (Frank Müller).

The winner of the best photo is:

Evelyne Peten (62) who has chalet in Lauenen and lives in London. She has had a long association with Gstaad as she was brought here as a baby when her grandfather bought a chalet. Then she went to school at Marie José and learnt to ski here.(see separate entry, Who's Who).

The 2nd winner in the top 5 is:

Stefan Jaggi (30), a Feutersoey carpenter who used a drone to take his photos.

The others include:

Hannes Schlögelhofer, a chef at the Post hotel Rössli;
Karin Bach (54), a farmer's wife and local guide;
Regula Hauswirth (32), a veterinarian;
Corinna Müller, a banker at the Saanen bank.

In the top 10 is:

Nadia Reichenbach (47), saleswoman and married with two children;
Rainier Donker (30), an Australian from Perth with family including grandparents living in Saanen and Chalberhön;
Francesca Herrmann (29), a chef in a nursing home in Saanen;
Pascal Bangerter (35), landscape gardener;
Kathrin Frautschi (56), sports teacher;
Elizabeth Riordan (70), an American and MIT alumni who has chalet in Rougemont.

In the top 15 is:

Janine Buchs (17), an apprentice at Raiffeisen bank;
Hans Bernasconi (70),a retired civil engineer;
Annekäthi Zingre (63), a former senior relationship manager of investment funds at Vontobel who lives in Gstaad and Geneva;
Deborah Walker (22), works for the Saanen bank;
Franz Rosskogler (70), former co-owner of Le Grand Chalet.

In the top 20 is:

Maria Rieder (54), a farmer's wife and photographer;
Daniela Giessbühler (43) a housewife from Zweisimmen;
Andy Kuenzi (45), a notary in Gstaad who lives in Schönried;
Sabine Reichenbach (43,) a social counsellor from Gstaad but lives in Bern.;
Uta Merzweiler (42), a mother of two children from Gsteig.

Photo by Evelyne Peten, the winner of the best photo.

Photo by Evelyne Peten, the winner of Photo Competition.

Photo by Stefan Jäggi, the 2nd winner in the top 5

Photo by Hannes Schlögelhofer.

Photo by Karin Bach

Opposite page photo by Rainier Donker.

Photos by Corinna Müller.

Photo by Nadia Reichenbach.

Opposite page photo by Janine Buchs.

Photos by Pascal Bangerter.

Photo by Maria Rieder.

Photo by Kathrin Frautschi.

Opposite page photo by Andy Kuenzi.

Photo by Franz Rosskogler.

TvG 41
2277
1.

Photo by Francesca Herrmann.

Opposite page photo by Annekäthi Zingre.

Photo by Elizabeth Riordan.

Photo by Deborah Walker.

Photo by Daniella Geissbuhler.

Photo by Hans Bernasconi.

Photo by Uta Merzweiler.

Photo by Werner Reichenbach.

Photo by Irene Kung.

Photo by Regula Hauswirth.

Index

A

Addor AG
Addor Heinz 157 Ruth, Daniela, Patrick, Marco 158, 159
Aghion Daniel 186
Alpine Cheese Dairy Tours 174
Andrews Dame Julie 13, 148
Anouilh Marina 96
Antonella 95
Armin Wehren AG 162
Azmoudeh Mehran 35

B

Bach Christoph 172
Bach Lorenz 19, 99
Bach Marcel 54, 115, 186
Bach Ueli and Karin 173
Baumann Hans Pieter 156
Baumer Erich and Louise 133 Tim and Linn 135
Behar Henri 198
Bettler Stephan 162
Bibliothek Saanenland / Library 156
Bircher Silvia 156
Blanco Manuel 144
Bohnenblust Thomas 143
Brand Hansueli Dominik Fabian 149
Bratschi, Robert, 85 Marlise 85 Elvira 85
Breuniger Klaus 160
Buure Metzg 85 AG
Braunsberg Andrew 60 Gabriele 61
Buchs Nik and Simon 141
Buure Metzg 85, 113

C

Cadonau 98
Camerana Christin Lang 74 192
Capuçon Renaud 182
CF Immobilier 164
Chaletbau Matti Architektur 161
Charly's 81
Chandris Loula 41, 189
Chnusper-Becke 81, 113
Collet Jeff 189
Coulter Amalia Clara 200, 201
Country Night 186
Credit Suisse 144
Crespi Antonia Bennassar 32
Czybik Mirka 121

D

Däpp Christoph 197
Délice 83 Heidi Sigrist-Wehren 83 Reto Sigrist 84
Dreyfus Pierre 183

E

Eagle Ski Club 41
Egger Walter 70, 155
Elsener Ermes 142
Elfen Denise 177
Enzian Keramik 103 Christine Baumgartner 103
Experience SA 153

F

Faux Raphael 151
Federer Roger 188 Mirka 188
Ferreira Pedro 136
Fix Karolos 75 Athina aka Ninetta 75
Foriel-Destezet Aline 29, 178, 179
Foriel-Destezet Phippe 30
Frei Werner 137

G

Galler Scheinerei AG 166
Galler Tom 166 Paul, Ruth, Marc 166
Genecand Pierre 17, 187
Giovanella Isabelle 104
Graff Laurence 76
Gstaad airport 154
Gstaad New Year Music Festival 184
Gstaad Yacht Club 190
Gudin Christophe 198
Guides Gstaad-Saanenland 203
Gymnasium Interlaken Gstaad branch 197

H

Hählen Bed & Baby 89 Ruedi 89 Christine 92
Hafner Caroline 184
Hauswirth Benz 62 Brigitte Leuenberger-Jaggi 62
Hauswirth, Martin 85, 113 Nicole 85, 113
Hauswirth Ueli 204, Christa 205
Hodler Urs 42, 189 Alice 43
Hoefliger Brigitte and Christian 130

Hotels

Alpenrose 126
Alpina 115
Arc-en-ciel 123
Bellevue 122
Ermitage 129
HUUS 119
Kernen 124
Olden 142
Palace 117
Sporthotel Victoria 127
Romantik Hotel Hornberg 130
Hublot Polo Gold Cup 118, 186

I

Iachia Manrico 72, 192
Intercoiffure Marti 105, Heinz Marti 105 Begoña Garcia 105

J

Jaggi architecture and Interior Design 159
Jaggi drogerie 16, 107 Peter Jaggi 16, 107 Hans Jaggi 16
Jaggi Stefan 207
J.Safra Sarasin Swiss Open Gstaad 187
John F. Kennedy International School 198

K

Kernen Bruno 124 Olga 125
Khalili Prof Nasser David 24
Koetser Daniel 23 Davia 123
Koetser David 53, 123
Koons Jeff 88
Kropf Aldo 98, 180 Marianne 98
Kultur Engagement 147
Kung Irene 49, 207
Küng-Marmet Bethli 41, 71
Kunz Urs 160

L

La Scarpa 109 Gabriele Gagneaux 109
Larosse Tess 42
Le Rosey (Institut) 198
Ledi Garage 149
Lutz Heiner 130
Local Farm Products 176
Low Patricia 88, 207

M

Maag Rudolf 123
Marmet Andre 172
Martin Louis and Elisabeth 164
Matti Christiane 123 Micheline 123
Matti Daniel 161
Matti Dominik 175
Matti Marianne 189
Matti, Ruedi 85
MC Avocats Sarl 152
MC Attorneys LLC 152
Meier, Anja 2
Menuhin Festival 177
Michalski-Hoffmann Vera 39
Mimran Jean-Claude 115
Mimran Nachson 21, 115
Molkerei 87
Mösching Forst 159
Mösching Martin 159 Benjamin and Karin 159 Mathias 159
Mount 10 AG 155
Müller Christoph 180
Müller Frank 146, 207
Müller Medien 146
Murat Princess Caroline 184
Museum Landwirtschaft 16

N

Naja Marwan 121
Nicod Bernard 47
Notz Brigitta 50
Notz Cedric 45 Andrea Brodin 46

O

Oehrli Tommy 127
 Fabienne 129
OSZ 129 198
Oschwald Christoph 156

P

Petten Evelyne 38, 207
Pictet Dariane 56
Photo Competition 207
Polanski Roman 13, 148
Prince Michel of Yugoslavia 30

R

R-Chocolate Boutique 79
Raaflaub Heidi 186, 189
Ravessoud Ombetta 66, 183
Restaurants
 16 Art Bar 141
 Brasserie/Wintergarden 138
 Grand Chalet 135
 Posthotel Rössli 137
 La Bagatelle 135
 Lac Retaud 139
 La Sarine 139
 Olden 142
 Sonnenhof 133
 Thai and Burger Takeaway 141
Romang Stefan 79
 Heidi 80
Rosscogler Franz 136
Rossignol-Franck Dominique 67
Roth-Reuteler Anita 203
Rougemont Interiors 94
Ryser René 87

S

Saanen Bank 145
Scarry Richard 63
 Fiona 65
 Olympia 65
Scherz Andrea 118
 Ernst 119
Schneider Rolf T. 152
Schopfer Heidi 171
Schuhhaus Romang 93
Schmid Laurenz 130
Schmid's Dorflade 102,
 Sarah 102
 Walter 102
Schönrich Cindy 192
Schwenter Caroline 181
Schwingen 142, 143
Sommets Musicaux de Gstaad 182
Speth Robert 34
 Susanne 34
Spillmann Hans Ruedi 37
Stahel Béatrice 152
Stähli Martin 198
Steiner Marc 155
Stocker Adrian 153
Stricker Blumen 108
 Andi Stricker 108

T

TopPharm Pharmacy 98
Tschanz Architektur AG 165
Tschanz Michael 165
Tschanz Hans-Ueli and Marléne 147
Treuthardt Irene 98
Turnels 175

U

UBS Gstaad 143

V

Valentino Garavani 13
von Allmen Jürg 145
von Grünigen Toni 58
 Barbara 59
von Siebenthal Michel and Carole 126
von Siebenthal Antina, Chantal and Yasmin 126
von Siebenthal, Robert 86
von Siebenthal Walter 172
 Andrea Sprenger 172
von Unger Urs 100

W

Wampfler Elisabeth 159
Wehren Andrea 81
Wehren Franz 139
Wehren Helen Ruedi 174
Weilguni Günter 111
Welland Tim 116
Wehren Philippe 162
 Eric 162
Widmer Conroy and Nadja 137
Willié Steve 136
Wittermann Lukas 182

Z

Zumstein Jakob 175
Zwahlen-Hueni 106
 Philipp Zwahlen 106